# Performance Riding
## Techniques

Published in June 2006

A catalogue record for this book is available
from the British Library

ISBN 1 84425 343 0

Library of Congress catalog card no. 2006921752

Haynes Publishing, Sparkford, Yeovil,
Somerset BA22 7JJ, UK
Tel: +44 (0) 1963 442030
Fax: +44 (0) 1963 440001
E-mail: sales@haynes.co.uk
Website: www.haynes.co.uk

Haynes North America, Inc.,
861 Lawrence Drive, Newbury Park,
California 91320, USA

Printed and bound by J.H.Haynes & Co Ltd,
Sparkford, Yeovil, Somerset BA22 7JJ, UK

This product is officially licensed by Dorna SL,
owners of the MotoGP trademark (© Dorna 2006)

**Editorial Director** Mark Hughes

**Design** Lee Parsons

**Photography** Gold and Goose

## DISCLAIMER

The riding techniques described in this book are intended only for high-speed riding on
a race track. Therefore they may not be suited to use on the public highway. The author
and publisher accept no responsibility for any accident resulting in injury or property
damage that might result from irresponsible, inappropriate, correct or incorrect use of any
techniques described in this book, other than for death or personal injury resulting from
their negligence. The author and publisher do not guarantee that readers will attain the
same high degree of riding skills that others have achieved by applying these techniques.
Supplementary notes, endorsements or quotes by noted riders who use these techniques
should not be taken as any guarantee as to safety or competency that might be gained,
but merely as personal comment. Always wear a proper helmet and full protective
clothing. Observe speed limits and the law when riding on the public highway.

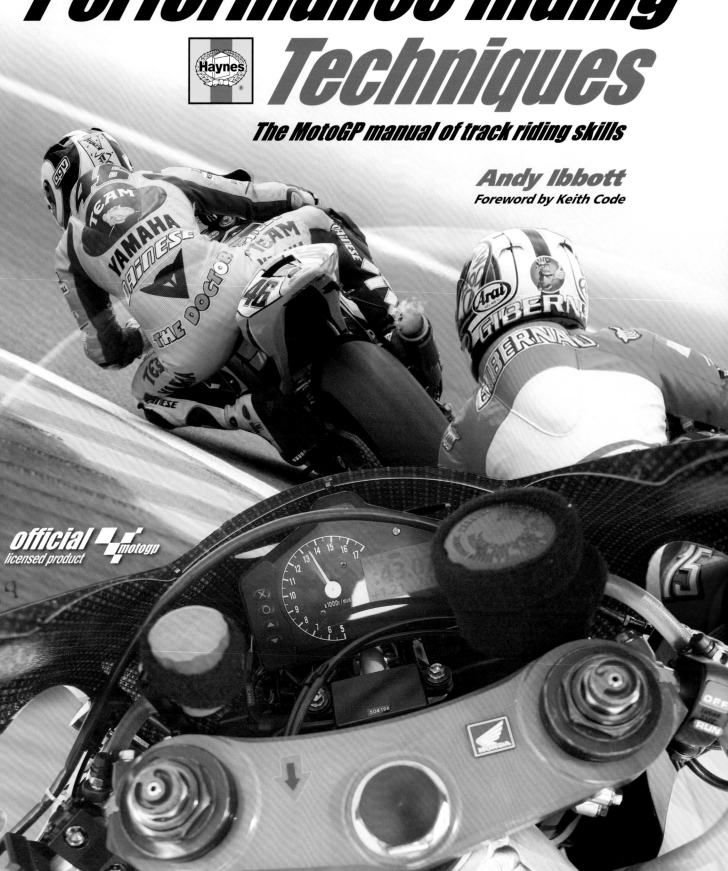

# Performance Riding Techniques

## Techniques

### The MotoGP manual of track riding skills

**Andy Ibbott**

Foreword by Keith Code

official licensed product motogp

# CONTENTS

# FOREWORD

Keith Code

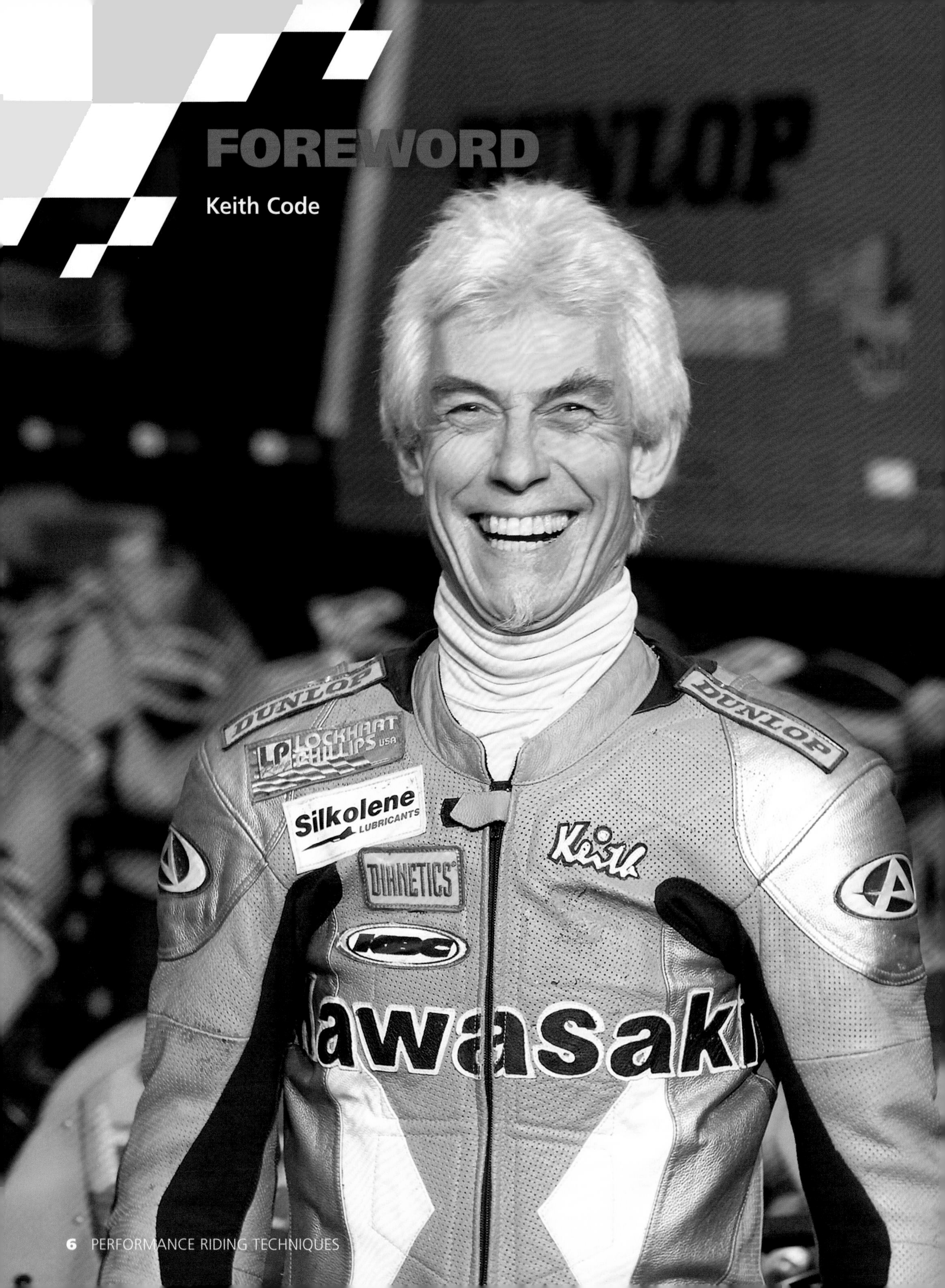

Road racing is a thrilling form of art. Its masters get and deserve all the adulation we heap upon them by virtue of their passion, commitment and the facile, almost miraculous use of their tools. The miracle is simply this: what we perceive as the hard-edged limits of riding become the tools of their trade and in their hands, fluid and malleable.

Indeed, what mortals perceive as the liabilities of riding our heroes see as assets and resources. What we see as barriers they re-shape and convert to their liberties. Traction, lean angle, speed, braking forces and acceleration are all metered by them with uncanny precision and consistency.

What would you give to be in the head and hands of Valentino Rossi for one lap? After restarting your heart, your choices would be a tail-between-the legs rout and abandonment of riding or a relentless crusade of seeking the skills to exercise the art on your own. If seeking the skills is your choice I applaud you and say you'll be pleased at the words herein.

Enter Andy Ibbott, who put pen to this work. Andy now has more experience training riders than anyone else in Europe by a factor of thousands and includes his personal coaching of Thomas Lüthi to last year's 125cc World Championship. His words contain some solid understanding of what it takes to make the bike cooperate with a rider.

In trying to sort out what makes the difference between us and them we see the true frailty of language. We can read and hear what they say but cannot feel what they feel. Here we have tried to fill in the gaps with some technical observations on how bikes work.

We bandy about the great buzz words of the sport like 'smooth', 'consistent' and 'confident', but what do they really mean in reference to: where the rubber meets the asphalt; where the hand winds on the throttle or presses on the bars or pulls and releases the levers or how our feet are on the pegs; where our behind sits in the saddle; where the eye embraces or rejects objects and spaces at a near-ballistic pace?

The simplicity of it all is astounding. On a motorcycle we do the same things as our heroes do: change speed and direction with the controls. That's all there is, no more and no less. When it goes right, speed and direction changes are precisely placed on the road and correctly metered, just the right amount. It's the same with errors. There are only five possible errors: changing speed or direction or both at the wrong time or in the wrong amount. No more and no less.

Wonderfully simple, isn't it? Sure, but where do you find that 20 seconds you need to be on the pace at your next race or track day? As you will see, our current crop of GP stars have an opinion on what they do and how they are doing it. You already know what it looks like. The purpose of this work is to gain more clues as to how it feels. This book is about what they say and how it looks in freeze-frame moments.

Put yourself in the pictures; fit their words into your own experiences; read between the lines. Try and filter out the barriers created by language and look at the potential for improvement in your own riding skills.

Discover the art.

**Keith Code**

Keith Code has coached more World Championship racers than anyone on this planet. He has written more books and articles on the subject of cornering a motorcycle than anyone else too. His ability to see the finest details and convert them into understandable, practical subjects and lessons is beyond belief. Often called the 'Cornering Guru', Code still applies himself to further discoveries in the art of cornering. Further articles and comments from him can be found in the forum section at www.superbikeschool.eu

# INTRODUCTION

Andy Ibbott

When Julian Ryder approached me at Phillip Island, Australia, with the idea to write this book, I have to say that I jumped at the opportunity.

"We want a book that's aimed at the track rider and aspiring racer," said Julian, "to help provide an insight and understanding as to how MotoGP riders do what they do, and to give riders a chance to follow in the footsteps of these amazing men."

These riders are at the top of their game, on the most amazing motorcycles you can imagine, carrying the highest cornering speeds and achieving the latest braking, the highest top speeds and the best lap times. And every year they get faster and faster, not only because of the development of their bikes, tyres and suspension, but also because they have an amazing ability to adapt and react to situations, mistakes and crises as they unfold in front of their eyes.

Interviewing these guys was a great help not only in writing this book but also in my own coaching knowledge. They all have different ways to deal with different situations. Some work, some don't. Some complement what you'll read on these pages, and some even contradict what's written here.

My aim in writing this book is to get you, the reader, the racer and track day enthusiast, to understand that if you want to go faster, get your lap times lower, then sheer balls isn't going to be enough. You're going to have to work at it, understand it, apply it and think about it if you're going to get faster.

Every racer and rider on this planet will come to a point when it seems impossible to go any faster. Fitting stickier tyres, tuning the engine further or getting a slightly better set-up seems to make little difference. No matter how hard you try your lap times just remain the same. MotoGP riders suffer from this too. In their case, they have a whole team of people behind them to help with the bike, their physical condition, their mental approach. But in the end it comes back to the rider to work out the challenges and get those last few tenths or even hundredths of a second. He'll be the one dealing with the forces generated from braking later, the punch as the bike accelerates out of the corner, to feel when he has or hasn't got grip, to get himself and the bike to work together to achieve the best lap time possible.

So, this book is dedicated to you, the rider and racer who's prepared to push personal limits to achieve the best possible lap time. It's a very selfish sport: only you can do the job in hand, but once you get it right, once you get the flow, once you go faster than you've ever gone before, then there's only one thing left to do...

Go faster still!

Enjoy it. It's life, it's living, it's fun.

**Andy Ibbott**
May 2006

## Readying man and machine for the off

**Getting the bikes ready for the coming weekend. Every part of the bikes will be checked over and serviced ready for the riders. Just setting up the garage takes a lot of time and effort. In this shot there are 12 people working – and it's only Wednesday.**

Having all parts of the bike clean and presentable might seem a little over the top, but it's important. If the working area is tidy and uncluttered, with all the tools and spares in the right place, everybody knows where everything is. It's more efficient but requires good preparation.

The bodywork on a MotoGP bike is made from the lightest, strongest carbon-fibre composite money can buy. It might seem a little crazy to swathe it in bubble wrap, but the graphics and paintwork aren't made from the strongest materials so keeping it all protected will ensure that the image of the team remains sharp and professional. It's a detail, but it shows the attention that a top team puts into every element of preparation.

## THE RIDER

Without doubt the rider, the fleshy bit on top of the bike, is the one thing that's going to make the most difference to how the bike underneath does its job. A good rider can overcome a lot of what the machine, a mechanic, suspension and engine tuning cannot. However, a good machine cannot overcome the limited abilities of the rider. Well, not strictly true: put me on Colin Edwards' bike and I'll ride fast, but put Edwards on my bike and I'll want to retire to a dark corner and hang my head in shame. Get the idea?

But with all that said, talent alone isn't going to be enough. This became obvious to me when I started to coach Thomas Lüthi, the 2005 125cc World Championship contender and eventual champion. At this level it's a combination of man, machine, mechanics, team manager – and a good supply of humour for those times when the whole team is up against it.

Shinya Nakano has these observations: "In the All Japan Championships I had a riding coach. He would watch me from the side of the track and he would say to change the body position or this or that. He helped a lot. He was a racer before. Then there are other people who come along who do not know racing and they tell me I am braking wrong. This is not good. You must find a coach you can trust – this is very important."

A rider will need to work on several areas if he's to achieve his ambitions, wherever they may be on the scale of things. Needless to say, a track-day addict in his 40s won't become a MotoGP World Champion no matter how much effort, time or money he invests – but he can be the best in his class, in his field, at his level.

"When you ride you should try and forget everything else," says Valentino Rossi. "Don't think about the rest of your life or the rest of the world. Try to forget all that and think only of the road or the track and the bike. It's not always easy to stay focused on the bike, sometimes you feel that one part of the brain rides the bike, thinks about the tyre, sees the road, but maybe the other part is thinking about a girl, a friend, a song."

So let's take a look at what you need to do to prepare yourself as well as possible.

## PHYSICAL TRAINING

This aspect mustn't be either over-rated or under-rated. Every rider needs to be fit. Some riders will be down at the gym at every single spare moment, or out riding motocross or mountain bikes. But research carried out by the British Sports Foundation demonstrates one thing very clearly – to get 'bike fit' you need to spend a lot of time actually riding a bike.

- Boots? Check
- Gloves? Check
- Leathers? Check
- Helmet? Check
- Well-placed sponsor logos? Check
- Grid girl? Check
- Bike? Check
- Chief engineer? Check
- OK, let's race!

"WHEN YOU RIDE YOU SHOULD TRY AND FORGET EVERYTHING ELSE. DON'T THINK ABOUT THE REST OF YOUR LIFE OR THE REST OF THE WORLD. TRY TO FORGET ALL THAT AND THINK ONLY OF THE ROAD OR THE TRACK AND THE BIKE. IT'S NOT ALWAYS EASY TO STAY FOCUSED ON THE BIKE, SOMETIMES YOU FEEL THAT ONE PART OF THE BRAIN RIDES THE BIKE, THINKS ABOUT THE TYRE, SEES THE ROAD, BUT MAYBE THE OTHER PART IS THINKING ABOUT A GIRL, A FRIEND, A SONG."
**VALENTINO ROSSI**

Loris Capirossi out on the slopes. Any sport or training that works your legs is good for riding a bike, particularly on track. The legs are the most important muscle group and the most powerful too for riding a race bike or track bike. Upper body training should be avoided but cardio-vascular training is needed. It's a fine balance that you need to get right.

Here's Chris Vermuelen on his training methods: "I don't do a lot of upper body training, I prefer light weights with slow repetitions. I do a lot of trails riding at home in Andorra. I can run as much as I want: I was a very fast middle-distance runner, over say ten kilometres, and very fit – but it didn't mean I was fit on a bike."

The muscle combinations we use on a bike and the order and manner we use them are unique – even to the point where riding a Motocross bike isn't the same as riding a track bike. It might sound obvious, but you have to realise that riding an off-road bike all winter won't keep you 100 per cent track fit.

Now, don't get me wrong, riding an off-road bike would be better than sitting in front of the PlayStation all winter learning tracks (more of that later), but it isn't the same as track riding. Also, as we've seen with many, many riders, Motocross brings a high risk of injury, and normally it's nasty: Troy Bayliss smashed his hand to bits, Neil Hodgson mangled his knee, Carl Fogarty damaged his leg. And Kevin Schwantz broke his wrist while mountain biking – an injury that arguably ended his GP racing career. Get the picture?

However, Colin Edwards likes to get on a Motocross bike to keep fit over the winter: "I do

lots of Motocross. After a whole season of MotoGP, I come home and a week later I do some Motocross and I'm aching like a Son of a Gun. Every muscle in my body is killing me and it's like, dude, how demanding is Motocross? I try not to get too crazy and make sure I don't injure myself."

Chaz Davies offers these comments: "I don't use the gym, but I road cycle quite a bit. I've never really done any weight training, always cardio-vascular. I find cycling is good but also there's not much better than riding Motocross bikes or Supermoto."

But why get fit in the first place? Every single rider on this planet has the same control actions and interactions with a motorcycle, and the list isn't long or complicated.

You use the throttle (wrist).

You use the front brake (right fingers).

You use the rear brake (right foot).

You use the clutch (left fingers).

You turn the bike left and right with the handlebars (arms).

You change gear (left foot).

And how much effort is involved in carrying out these actions?

Acceleration requires a small twist of the wrist. Braking requires light pressure from your fingers. Look at changing gear, or changing direction. The effort required isn't massive.

No, you need to get fit to deal with the *forces* that act on your body as a result of these small actions. Braking hard generates an enormous amount of force that tries to throw you off the bike. A good 600 can do the same with acceleration – let alone a tuned 1000, a thoroughbred 250 GP bike or a monster-carbon-brake-shod-250bhp-plus-MotoGP-mutha. Turning the bike also creates its own set of forces.

All this explains why we need to get down to the gym, get running and build up our stamina – but even then we must be careful how and what we train.

Overall it's stamina that has to be the aspect at the top of the list. For myself, having ridden endurance races, short-blast 600 Sportsport club races and long-duration Nationals, I was surprised to find that the short races were the ones that took the most out of me. It's the same on a track day. You get 20 minutes to dial it all in and then rest for the next 40 minutes before the next burst.

"On the bike you need to stay concentrated and relaxed, and to do that you need to have enough air for the brain," says Valentino Rossi.

So training should be based around stamina and flexibility. By the end of the winter you should look like an athlete, not a ripped and torn muscle-bound beach bum. One area to watch is your forearms: make sure that you're very light with the work as too much will give you problems with arm pump, a nasty way of your body telling you that you've overdone it.

Forearm pump is the bane of many racers, even to the point that some have a carpal tunnel operation to open up the muscle's sleeve so that the muscle can expand more. A less drastic solution, however, is to use the legs more effectively and efficiently, as forearm pump occurs when the rider hangs on too hard with his arms and doesn't use his legs enough.

"I use my legs a lot to keep my body weight forward on the bike," says James Ellison. "I only get forearm pump when I ride Motocross bikes. They say it takes a full year of riding Motocross bike to get over forearm pump, to the point where you can do an entire Motocross race without suffering.

"I don't do any upper body work at all and I don't use weights. When I train over the winter I do core work, use one of these big gym balls and only do things where I use my own body weight. You can only get bike-fit riding a bike. It doesn't matter how much training you do over the winter, you end up knackered after the first test."

Would you be fit enough to ride a MotoGP bike for 40 minutes in a race? The forces that a rider's body has to cope with are extraordinary and the training he does needs to match the demands made by braking, accelerating and cornering. But it's not just the top racers who must train: using a 1000cc road bike for a track day will also make demands on your fitness.

Colin Edwards deep in thought. What's his plan for the coming race? To win? For sure, but how to win is the real question. Does he need a good start and then establish a gap no-one can bridge? Is he thinking of running hard tyres and making up ground at the end of the race? Is he thinking about the start and where he wants to be in the first corner? Or is he thinking about his pet badger?

"Legs are the biggest part of training for sure," says John Hopkins. "I cycle maybe five days a week and do 30 to 40 miles per day, and two days of running around four to five miles each day."

Thomas Lüthi takes his gym training a stage further: "I do a lot of work not only on the body for stamina but also for hand-to-eye co-ordination and reaction times."

Running or cycling provides a good work-out. Light weights, a rowing machine and a stair-climber also all help to achieve your goal.

Remember that body fitness also means that you have a fit and agile mind. As Loris Capirossi states: "In the beginning I did not really do a lot of training, only the things that I like, Motocross but not a lot. Now I do a lot of training and I don't like some of it. Trials bikes are good and I like that for the balance."

## TRAINING SUPPLEMENTS

The rules on drugs are becoming increasingly complicated and the use of supplements in training is more and more common-place. It's becoming more difficult to see where the line should be drawn. While this whole area hasn't been as much of an issue in motorcycle racing as it is in athletics, the riders are nevertheless subject to random testing. If you're in any doubt about training supplements, the best advice is to avoid them completely.

## MENTAL APPROACH

Focused. We hear this a lot on the television, and we often see the word in books, magazines and newspapers. It's true that each and every rider should be focused before going out on the track and riding. But focused on what? A track day rider will have a different focus from a racer. A racer will have different focus during testing compared with when he's racing or practising.

Some racers have a mental coach or sports psychologist, but others don't think it's worth it. James Ellison is one: "No, I tried that. No-one knows what's going on inside your head except you."

The point is, whether or not you have a sports psychologist, you must focus on something, and for your riding it has to be something very precise, very exact and very refined. Just saying to yourself 'I wanna go faster' isn't going to do the trick.

"The rider is a big part of the motorcycle, so you need to understand that you're a part of the bike," says Valentino Rossi. "It's not the bike and the rider – both need to be like one thing. You also need to think about having a good relationship with the bike and making a direct rapport with it. Try to understand what she

wants from you, so you can ride the bike differently, especially if you want to make good of different settings, different tyres and other modifications. You always need to arrive at this situation step by step. If you think well and go step by step, you should be able to have a 100 per cent feeling with your bike."

Focusing on a riding technique, such as throttle application, and trying to get it on a little sooner is what focus is about. Saying that you need to work on your line in turn X is focus. Deciding that you need to change the way you brake for a session or the way you hang off is focus. It's goal-driven. Without a goal you just have track time, and worse still it's wasted track time.

"I don't really prepare myself for a race," observes Chris Vermeulen. "I'm very relaxed before a race. I'm as chilled out as I would be for any other session. I find if I think about it too much I stress about it and then I'll be off the mark for the first few laps."

My mentor, Keith Code, author of the best-selling *Twist of the Wrist* books, founder of the California Superbike School and riding coach to racing legends like Wayne Rainey, John Kocinski and Scott Russell, once told me that track time was like toilet paper – the more you had the more you wasted. If you just had one sheet left then you became very efficient. I've never forgotten that and it's absolutely true. It's better to do a single 20-minute session and improve one thing in your riding than to spend all day just blasting around banging your head against a brick wall not getting any better.

So make a plan for the day of riding you have ahead of you. We'll talk more later in the book about what you can practise and how, but for now, as part of your plan – have a plan.

It's very easy to under-think or over-think your riding, and as a result not get the satisfaction you want from a good race or track day blast.

It's also very easy to practise the same old mistakes time and time again and never improve your riding, only improve your ability to scare yourself silly as the mistakes you make just occur at a higher and higher speed.

When was the last time you really, *really* thought about what you were trying to achieve in a corner?

We see people spend thousands of pounds on tuning their engines, hundreds of pounds tweaking suspension and yet more money on stickier tyres – but all to little or no avail much of the time.

Ah-ha, Rossi is coming! So what will your plan be now? To follow him for a lap to try and reduce your lap times? To get a tow down the straight because his bike is faster than yours? To tag on for as many laps as possible to see his lines? To see where he's braking compared to you? Just to follow him would be a mistake as you wouldn't be learning. However, how long could you follow him for, yet still have enough attention left to be able to learn from him and not exceed your personal limits?

Understanding what you're doing or not doing, and when, will produce far more long-term improvement in your riding than you could possibly imagine.

You can start with some fairly simple questions. When do I start to apply the throttle in a corner? What am I looking at when I peel in? Do I look too close to the front of the bike?

Without a series of questions to ask yourself, then you'll never make significant leaps forward in how you ride and in your level of confidence in cornering your bike.

So what should you be asking yourself? In a nutshell there are two areas to address. The first is your physical interaction with the bike. The second is what you look at or don't look at while you're riding.

It's the how, the when, the what and the why that results in a good, confident, controlled corner rather than a frantic snatch and grab of the controls to survive a corner. When you've completed a corner, ask yourself how it felt. Was it smooth? Why? What did you look at? When did you look at it? All these questions for every corner will make you smoother and more confident – and a better rider. We can't change what we don't know and if you don't question your riding then you'll never know how to improve it.

## PLANNING

Now let's take a look at the next area that needs your attention. You're going racing and you need to get ready for the weekend ahead of you.

Again, a plan is good and helps you to get focused. Have you packed your ear plugs, spare gloves and licence? Have you got all your kit stored and ready to go or is it a last-minute rush after you get home from work? Do you have a decent, fully stocked tool kit? Do you keep all your paperwork in a folder?

But what about the preparation a rider has to do to race, to win, to beat his team-mate – this is a whole different area.

All riders have little rituals, set ways of doing things before the flag. Some do it in the garage, some in the motorhome, some on the start line, some on the warm-up lap – a ritual is a good thing as it tells you you're getting ready for the challenge ahead.

John Hopkins says he spends a lot of time thinking about the tracks: "I try to spend at least an hour a day going through the track in my head. I try and think about all my lines throughout the whole circuit, going back and forth looking at braking markers and stuff like that so that when you show up you are prepared and immediately you are good on the

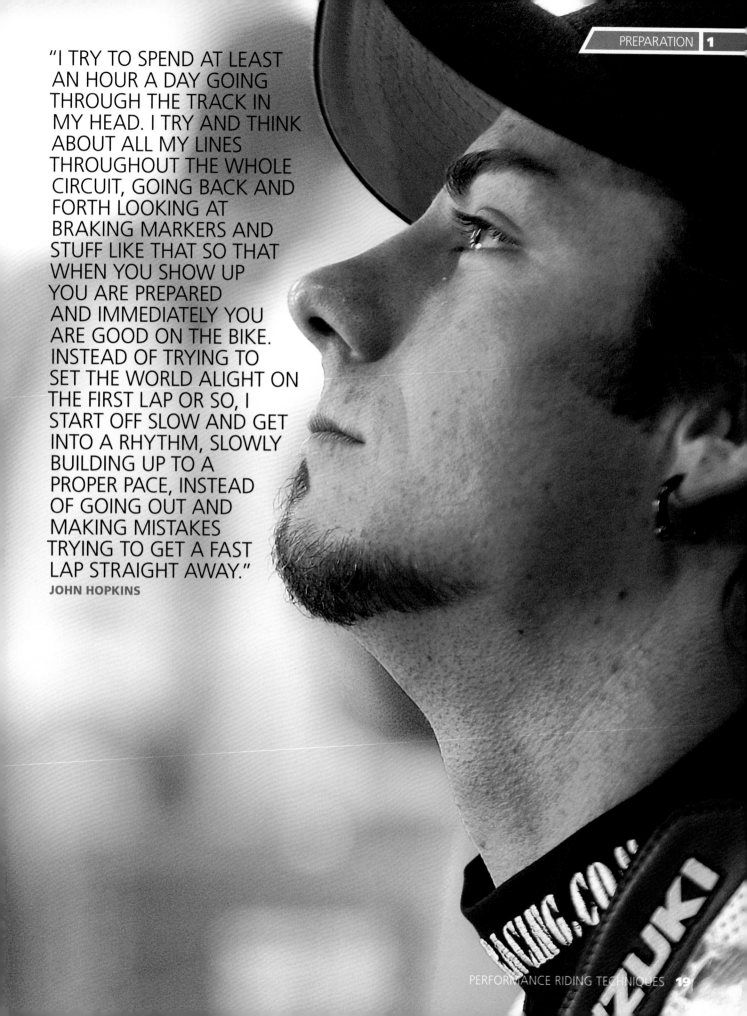

"I TRY TO SPEND AT LEAST AN HOUR A DAY GOING THROUGH THE TRACK IN MY HEAD. I TRY AND THINK ABOUT ALL MY LINES THROUGHOUT THE WHOLE CIRCUIT, GOING BACK AND FORTH LOOKING AT BRAKING MARKERS AND STUFF LIKE THAT SO THAT WHEN YOU SHOW UP YOU ARE PREPARED AND IMMEDIATELY YOU ARE GOOD ON THE BIKE. INSTEAD OF TRYING TO SET THE WORLD ALIGHT ON THE FIRST LAP OR SO, I START OFF SLOW AND GET INTO A RHYTHM, SLOWLY BUILDING UP TO A PROPER PACE, INSTEAD OF GOING OUT AND MAKING MISTAKES TRYING TO GET A FAST LAP STRAIGHT AWAY."

**JOHN HOPKINS**

Valentino Rossi 'praying' to his bike. He does this every single time he goes out to ride – one of his little rituals to prepare for the job ahead. Like most racers, he has many of them if you watch him closely. Some are based on superstition, others just on preparation and habit. But all of them, once ingrained, will be vital to a rider's build-up to a race.

bike. Instead of trying to set the world alight on the first lap or so, I now start off slow and get into a rhythm, slowly building up to a proper pace, instead of going out and making mistakes trying to get a fast lap straight away.

"I've always done this to some degree but working with Randy Mamola has really helped. Even when I started in 500cc GPs it was a big jump from Formula Xtreme, so I did every little thing I could to improve my riding. I'd be studying tracks on the PlayStation long before I actually showed up at them."

I was always incredibly anxious when I was in the collecting area – nerves don't begin to describe how I felt. It was all part of the rush, the reason I was there, this was it, to the finish, better get ready. I would talk to no-one: I would find a quiet part of the collection area to wait by myself. Visor down.

And yet the very moment my front wheel hit the track, the instant I was on the circuit for real, all the nerves went away.

When the nerves start varies from rider to rider: with some it's just a few minutes before the race, for others it's a few hours. For James Ellison the nerves come and go: "I first get a kick about half an hour before I walk down to the garage. I start to get excited and then when I get on the bike I get nervous. Around the grid

I'm fine until the countdown boards appear – then it stays with me all the way round on the warm-up lap, and at the start of the race, and then for the first two or three laps – and then I start to settle down again."

And as any racer's partner will tell you, the stress was in fact already there before that kick of adrenaline arrived – short tempers are common in the paddock. I think every racer suffers from stress, but not all show it; some start to feel it early in the build-up to the event, others on the day. And it's normally those closest to you that get the lion's share of it. In my case, chucking all the contents of my race van out over the paddock was not an uncommon situation when I couldn't find something I needed.

Shinya Nakano gets excited before the race: "In the motor home before the race – whaaaah! But Valentino always looks so normal before the race. I think he knows how to handle this kind of pressure."

How you ever noticed how GP racers have everything in a particular place, easy to find and normally put there by a team member who has that precise job – to make sure everything is ship-shape and Bristol fashion. Can you imagine the fracas if Rossi's gloves were in the wrong part of the garage? You might not see it on TV but there would be hell to pay for someone.

Chaz Davies gets his kicks on the track: "Yes, I get a rush normally when I do a lap that feels really on the limit and I know it was fast, and come out of corners getting on the gas knowing that the bike could spit you off at any moment but it doesn't."

Look at each racer in the pits. Rossi has a whole range of habits, some for him, some to throw the opposition off guard (more of that later). He always watches the start of the 125 race. He 'prays' to his bike. He puts on his gloves in a certain way, he pulls the pants out of his arse as he leaves pitlane, adjusts his wedding tackle, and then pulls his pants out of his arse again on the start/finish line. As habit, attitude and focus go, this boy has the lot.

Some riders like to jump around their motorhomes to loud music – the great Wayne Rainey used to do this. It's a way of getting shot of all that nervous energy, all that pent-up adrenaline, and bringing the mind to the job in hand.

Of course you could be like Aussie Chris Vermeulen "I don't get an extra kick of adrenaline – it's just the same every time I go out on the bike. It comes when I put on my helmet and gloves"

Find your way of getting to grips with the fact that you could die in the next few minutes, you could get seriously injured or crippled – but you could also have the ride of your life, in the zone, cooking on gas, and come back into the pits knowing you've just lived life to the full in the last few exhilarating minutes.

## NATURAL SELECTION

The way racing works is a natural selection process. OK, some of a rider's progress can be influenced by the money a team needs to raise to keep in the game, but any rider will have to go through a series of levels and challenges to make it to the top.

At the broad bottom of this huge pyramid are track days. This is where a lot of riders can start to hone their basic track skills and get an idea of what's needed and if they can or even want to start the progression to racing. Here you can work up from the slow group to the intermediate one and then the fast one. Your progress here is one way of gauging how you would do in a race.

Even if his team bought him more comfortable underwear, Valentino Rossi would still be performing this little ritual on his way out of pitlane. It's not about comfort – it's about preparation.

"ON THE BIKE YOU NEED TO STAY CONCENTRATED AND RELAXED, AND TO DO THAT YOU NEED TO HAVE ENOUGH AIR FOR THE BRAIN."
VALENTINO ROSSI

Marco Melandri has earned the right to be at the highest level. Whether you come through the Superbike, Supersport or 125/250 routes, you'll have earned your spurs, your right to compete with the best the world can offer.

## GO RACING

The next level up from doing lots of track days is to actually go racing.

"Stick with it," advises John Hopkins. "Take the good times with the bad times and the horrible times, but at the end of the day you've just got to stick it with."

You'll need to start at club level, the roots of racing. This is where you'll get your first lessons in racecraft. It won't be like a track day: the gloves will be off and you'd better get used to a lot of bikes being around you – and all of them will be after that piece of track you've set your sights on! It'll be a mad dash to the finish line and you'll have very little time to dial yourself in as practice sessions are short 10-minute affairs first thing in the morning.

Colin Edwards has some sound advice for you: "Have a massive bank account! It costs money and when you chuck one down the road you'll find this out real quick."

In the UK you'll need to wear a bright orange or yellow novice jacket until you've completed ten race meetings on three different tracks within a three-year period. You then progress to a Clubman's licence and you won't have to wear your novice jacket any more.

## ROAD RACE (UK)

### ■ FIRST-TIME APPLICANTS

All first-time Road Race applicants in the UK are required to complete a competitor training course and also provide evidence of competence to ride a motorcycle before a competition licence can be issued.

The competitor training course, which is held at ACU House, is classroom-based and designed to familiarise applicants with the basic safety and organisational requirements needed to participate in Road Racing.

### ■ NOVICE

Entry level for persons not holding a Category A Motorcycle Road Licence. An orange jacket will be required (supplied by the ACU on request at a cost of £7.00 including VAT).

### ■ INTERMEDIATE NOVICE

Entry level for persons holding a Category A Motorcycle Road Licence, a photocopy of which must be enclosed with your application (please do not send original documents). An orange jacket will be required (supplied by the ACU on request at a cost of £7.00 including VAT).

### ■ UPGRADING TO CLUBMAN

Riders must supply evidence on their competitor record card(s) of competing satisfactorily during the last 3 years in at least 10 separate meetings on at least 3 different venues.

Only one successful attendance at a recognised training school will count as one meeting/signature towards upgrading.

### ■ UPGRADING TO NATIONAL

Riders must supply evidence on their competitor record card(s) of competing and finishing in the top 50 per cent during the past three years in at least ten separate meetings on at least four different venues.

National racing is the highest level you can apply yourself to in your country and if you think about the number of riders on the grid (40-odd in most classes) then you'll be against the best the country can offer in that particular class. The competition, therefore, has just moved up a peg or two, and even if you were the best in your club races you may get a bit of a shock when the flag drops for your first race at this level.

### ■ UPGRADING TO INTERNATIONAL

Riders must have completed a full year of racing at National level, then they are automatically upgraded to an International licence.

Now you can play with the really big boys from right across the globe. Well done: you've reached the highest of the high, the best of the best.

### ■ ACU TRAINING COURSE FOR ROAD RACE LICENCE APPLICANTS (UK)

The ACU Training Course (ACU-T Course) is classroom-based and designed specifically for you. The purpose of the course is to ensure that you understand the basic safety and organisational requirements to participate in road racing. Before any new licence can be issued, you must satisfactorily attend the course and pass the multiple-choice test.

● The ACU Training Course is held every Monday, at ACU House, Rugby except on Bank Holidays. The course starts at 11.00am and concludes by approximately 3.00pm.

● You will have one year, from the date you attend the ACU Training Course, to apply for your competition licence.

● You must also prove your competence to ride a motorcycle. You can do this in one of the following ways:

● You can obtain a certificate of competence from a recognised track-based training school and attach this to your competition licence application.

● If you hold a valid Class A DVLA driving licence or valid CBT Certificate, a copy should accompany your competition licence application.

● If you have held an ACU competition licence for a minimum of one year for any off-road

discipline, a copy, along with a result sheet from a race, should accompany your competition licence application.

● But before you apply, consider the wise words of Loris Capirossi about young riders.

"First of all there is pressure. This is not a game. Because if someone is thinking I'll go racing – no. This is a job – but not a bad job. The worrying thing is we have a lot of young riders now. I started many years ago when I was 17. Before I started there were not many young riders, most came along when they were 22, 23, 24. But sometimes the riders come in too early and lose everything. When you come in too early it's not so easy to come into the World Championships – we have many strong riders and it's easy to lose your confidence and then your career."

### BIKE PREPARATION

Whether you're a serious racer or just like having fun on track days, getting your bike ready for the job in hand is an important part of the process. While a MotoGP rider has a whole group of people fettling the bike to get the best from it, you'll have to do your own work – and it's a good education to do it. The paddock will be alive with little tips and tricks that you can do to your bike without having to spend thousands of

Get to the highest levels and you'll have a whole team of technicians and engineers to work on your bike. No dirty hands now! However, until then it's a good grounding to do your own work on your bike. It will educate you and help you to acquire a deeper understanding of how it all works. This could become valuable in later seasons when you have to give clear and accurate feedback to your team.

When you take off all the bodywork, you can get to the important parts of the bike that need preparing before each and every race. The more you can learn about the workings of the bike, the more you understand how to ride it to its full potential.

pounds on tuning the engine. Some of the advice will make working on the bike easier, other aspects will give you a small competitive advantage.

For my first season in the 600 Supersport class, I ran the bike on stock rear suspension and – on the very first outing – on road tyres. The tyres were certainly a mistake as halfway through the race I ended up in another hospital with another broken bone. Note to self and to you, dear reader: never, ever skimp on your tyres. Anything else, but not your tyres.

Basic preparation of your bike for the track will mean you will need to ditch that lovely ABS plastic bodywork and road-going paraphernalia. In the old days it was for safety as the lights were glass and would shatter and leave sharp shards all over the track, causing further accidents and injuries. It was also done for weight-saving as the plastic was very heavy. Nowadays it's so your bike can look cool and like a proper racing bike, with more room for sponsor's stickers. As ever, it's also a damned sight cheaper to replace and repair when you crash. Do note that phrase 'when you crash': it's gonna happen and even the best in the world do it on a regular basis, whether it's their fault or the result of a mistake by another rider.

Take off everything that will have no use on

the track. Lights, indicators, number-plate holders and pillion seat units – unless your name is Randy Mamola and you have a two-seater thrill machine with which to scare the heck out of unsuspecting VIP guests.

With your bike in your garage looking very naked and bare and not worth the money you paid for it, you now need to go over the other points and get an introduction to lock wire. Lock wire is used to keep nuts and bolts in place to make sure that the fluid behind them stays in place and not all over the track. You'll need to drill a hole in the nuts or bolts and then drill another close by so you can run the wire from one place to the other so that it all stays tight. Track day riders don't need to do this, but racers will.

You'll need to place a bottle to catch any overflowing fluids that may also make a run for it. The radiator overflow and the engine breather are the two that you'll definitely need to deal with.

Items to wire include but are not limited to:
Sump plug
Radiator cap
Oil filter
Some riders also lock wire the brake caliper bolts although this isn't needed in the regulations.

With that done you should now fit anything the rule book demands such as a 'shark fin' to protect your pinkies from the rear sprocket and chain. This, erm, shark fin-shaped protector goes on the bottom of the swing arm near the rear sprocket and most production-based bikes have a factory-fitted lug to assist fitting.

Now remove the side stand and – heaven forbid – centre stand if fitted (hell, what class are *you* racing in?) and fit a set of paddock stand bobbins for the shiny new paddock stand that you've just spent too much money on instead of getting one off eBay.

Now take your naked bike outside and give it a damned good clean. You will be amazed at how many loose, missing or knackered items you'll come across as you do this. And get into the habit of doing this each time you finish a day at the track, whether you're racing or track-daying – it could quite literally save your bacon one day.

Now, other things to consider. Did you buy your bike new and convert it to track use? Or did you buy a bike that was already converted?

Either way, while you have the bike in bits it's a good time to get all the moving parts lubed up. Take out the forks, undo the headstock and pack a whole load of new grease in there; do the same to the rear shock linkage and for the swing arm. Do this even if the bike is new as you'll be shocked how little grease the manufacturers put in. Do the same to all the bits you will remove on a regular basis: brake calipers, wheel spindles, chain adjusters and so on.

Of course, you can say: 'That's too much hard work, I just wanna ride' But every little bit of attention to detail helps.

Time to put it all back together and fit your new race bodywork. Race bodywork comes in two flavours. Good, easy to fit and with marks for the holes you're going to need to drill. Or bad, ill-fitting and needing to be hacked to get it to fit.

Saving a few pounds on bodywork is sometimes an ill-conceived plan.

It will also be wise to fit some crash protectors as you're not in a MotoGP team with a huge budget. It could save you a set of uppers at some point or at least mean you might get away with just repairing them instead of replacing them.

Your radiator will need to be drained and filled with plain old water. You're not allowed to have antifreeze in it as it makes the track too slippery should you puncture it during a crash.

Time to think about the engine. To tune or not to tune? I know that sounds mad – no tune? Well, I've seen a lot of riders who spend thousands of pounds on an

Every time a MotoGP bike is used, the technicians will strip it down and prepare it again for the next session. The more extensively the bike is tuned, the more looking after it will need. Turn-key racing is really limited to the more basic classes, and really only to four-strokes as two-strokes tend to require more maintenance.

Preparing for the rain. Not only will the tyres have been changed to wets, but different-sized rims will have been fitted as well in the quest for the best grip in slippery conditions. The suspension will also have been softened as the forces created are lower in wet conditions. Notice in this shot that the brakes have been changed: the D'Antin team has fitted steel discs because they give a more progressive feel than carbon discs.

engine tune only to be beaten by a CB500 on a track day. I would strongly advise a race pipe (cheaper to replace) and associated Power Commander before going for the full-on tune – at least until you can judge if you really do need another 20bhp.

A lot of club racing bikes really only need to be geared properly for a particular track – and then the need for more power becomes less of an issue. You can gain more from better throttle control than another 10 ponies. When the Suzuki GSXR1000 first hit the Superbike scene, a lot of riders were getting nearly 200bhp of unusable power. John Reynolds is alleged to have asked Suzuki to detune the bike and as a result he rode faster because he had power that was usable.

So do you really need your bike tuned? If you bought it tuned then it's good to get it looked over before the season starts to make sure that:

A. It's what you thought you'd bought and not yet another replica of some famous racer's bike.

B. It doesn't go pop mid-season because the inlet valves were knackered.

Where possible buy a set of wheels with discs so you can have a set of wet-weather tyres on standby. Mind you, once you've bought them you'll never race or ride in the rain again...

Make sure the brake pads are in good nick and are racing pads as they're more resistant to fade under heavy use. Also make sure you've replaced the brake fluid for some new stuff at the beginning of the season.

Get your spares kit together and a tool kit containing everything you think you could ever need. It's always better to have too much than too little. Pack another box full of all the lubes you need.

Take another box or bag with spare gloves and a spare helmet as these are the items most likely to be written off in an accident – something that *will*, not might, happen.

One area often overlooked is the positioning of your levers.

Having your levers set correctly can make all the difference to how well and how confidently you can

**Make sure that your levers are set at the correct angle. They should be positioned so you can use them with minimum effort. If you have to contort your foot to change gear, then the lever should be moved. Having the lever set too high can cause you to suffer from wrist and forearm fatigue.**

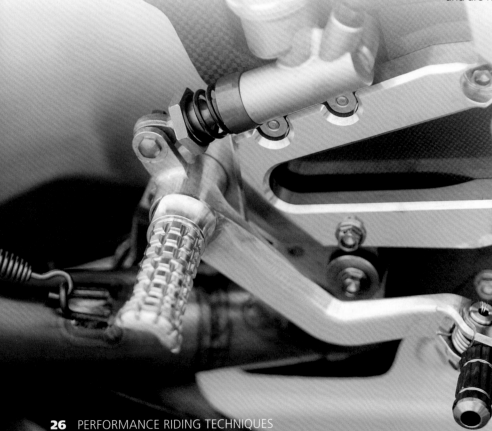

control your bike in all situations. It's also something we never consider and adapt to frighteningly quickly. You can jump on a strange bike, feel the brake lever is set too high and adapt to that within one lap!

The old journalistic cliché 'the controls fall easily to hand' has a ring of truth to it, and your adjustments should include the rear brake and gear shifter too. If your levers are in the wrong position it can hinder your ability to have full control over them at any speed.

For example, if your front brake lever is set too high, then you'll find it hard to react efficiently if you need to brake in an emergency. You'll also have difficulty simultaneously braking and blipping the throttle on the downshift, and you could well end up with aching, even painful, wrists as a result of the contorted position your hand must adopt. And this can come about if the lever is as little as 5mm too high.

Too low is just as much of a problem. For example, if you have your gear shift lever too low, then you'll find it difficult to shift up and you may have to move your foot or even take it right off the footpeg to make the change to another gear. This can make you unstable on the bike and create a handling problem all on its own!

If the rear brake lever is too high, then you're more likely to over-brake in an emergency situation, and if it's set too low you'll probably under-brake. Of the two, too low seems to be the better option...

And the clutch – the most frequently used control action after the throttle. Like the front brake lever, too high or too low a setting will cause you to be inefficient in the way you feed it out, which can seriously affect your race starts.

And this leaves the most used control action – the throttle. Too much slack in the cable and you'll never use the full potential of the engine because you'll only get 95 per cent of the throttle opening unless you take two handfuls to get the cable to the stop. Too little slack and you'll need the throttle control of a MotoGP riding god at low speed – to be able to squeeze it gently enough would be like taking a dummy from a sleeping baby. Too much and the interface between the ground and the front wheel could be very wide...

Ideally you need the levers set so that you can use them with minimal effort. Front brake and clutch levers should be set so that you can draw a straight line from your fingertips through your wrist to your elbow when you assume your most common riding position.

For foot levers, again make sure that you have the least amount of foot movement to operate them. Happy adjusting!

It's a good idea to have a small folder for all your race paperwork, including your race licence

On MotoGP bikes you can even make adjustments on the move. The small dial that can be seen above the handlebar grip allows adjustments to the feel of the front brake.

and any medical notes and medical cover that might be required. Oh, and your dog tags. These should bear your name, date of birth and blood group. When you finally make it to the MotoGP paddock, you'll no longer need to wear them as the organisers have your complete medical records on file.

## CHEATING

If you have to cheat then you really shouldn't be in the sport. It's one thing to bend the rules but it's an entirely different story to break them. Unfortunately at club level cheating is rife, as the scrutineers can't always make a full inspection of the bikes because there are simply so many of them to be examined over a weekend. And so cheating can go unchecked, the situation relying on the honesty of the competitors. Big-bore kits on bikes, slicks cut with a road race pattern, illegal ECUs or wiring looms – these are just some of the things people will do to seek an unfair advantage over their fellow competitors.

And even at national levels it goes on. Of course, the general rule is the higher you go the less cheating occurs as the checks and measures and fines and loss of credibility increases. In MotoGP the rules are there to encourage as much experimentation as possible so cheating isn't an issue.

"STICK WITH IT, AND THAT'S IT. TAKE THE GOOD TIMES WITH THE BAD TIMES AND HORRIBLE TIMES, BUT AT THE END OF THE DAY YOU'VE JUST GOT TO STICK WITH IT."

**JOHN HOPKINS**

## KNOW YOUR FLAGS!

This is how the track marshals communicate with you while you're in the heat of battle. It's very simple and works extremely well in all forms of motorsport. If you're riding around and not sure what the flag being waved at you means it could ultimately cost you or another rider his or her life. It's serious and you should know them all off by heart!

Flag rules can vary slightly from country to country, but the list here gives the flag rules currently in use in the MotoGP class across the world.

They are taken from the FIM Road Racing World Championship MotoGP handbook.

**GREEN** Track is clear. Used on the warm-up laps so the riders can see the marshals' points and after a yellow flag has been shown to inform the rider he is clear of the incident.

**YELLOW/RED STRIPES** Adhesion affected by any reason *other than* rain.

**WHITE/RED CROSS (DIAGONAL)** Drops of rain on this section of track.

**WHITE/RED CROSS AND YELLOW/RED STRIPES** Rain on this section of track.

**BLUE** Rider about to be overtaken. In a practice session the rider must keep his line then slow to allow overtake. In a race the rider must allow a pass as soon as possible.

**CHEQUERED** Race finished.

**YELLOW** A delayed start and danger ahead, no overtaking. Penalties for overtaking on a yellow. In practice that lap time will be cancelled. In a race the rider must drop back to his position before the overtake as decided by Race Control. Failure to do so will result in a 60km/h pitlane ride-through.

**WHITE FLAG** Rider can change machines.

**RED** Return slowly to the pits.

**BLACK AND BIKE NUMBER** Go to the pits on that lap. Your race is finished.

**BLACK WITH AN ORANGE DISK AND A BIKE NUMBER** Mechanical problem, leave the track immediately.

# ACCELERATING

**Wheelies may impress your girlfriend, but they just waste time**

When the front wheel is in the air, the bike isn't driving as hard as it could. Some of the power of the engine is being used to lift the front of the bike. To see just how much power is being lost here, grab hold of your bike's front wheel and lift it up a few centimetres!

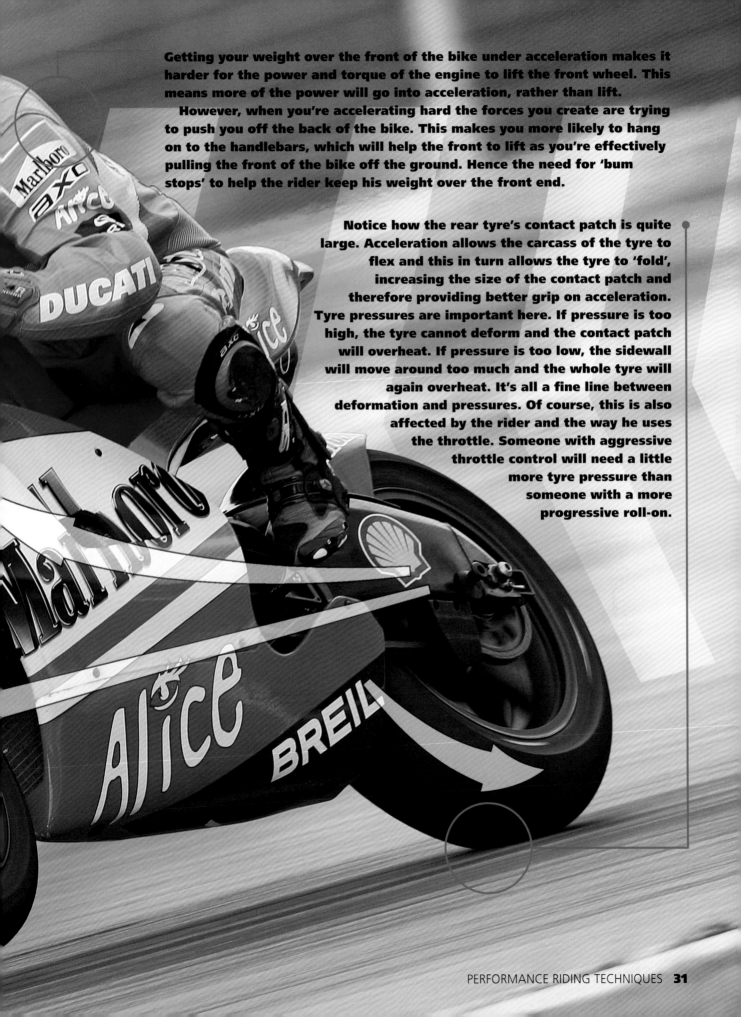

Getting your weight over the front of the bike under acceleration makes it harder for the power and torque of the engine to lift the front wheel. This means more of the power will go into acceleration, rather than lift.

However, when you're accelerating hard the forces you create are trying to push you off the back of the bike. This makes you more likely to hang on to the handlebars, which will help the front to lift as you're effectively pulling the front of the bike off the ground. Hence the need for 'bum stops' to help the rider keep his weight over the front end.

Notice how the rear tyre's contact patch is quite large. Acceleration allows the carcass of the tyre to flex and this in turn allows the tyre to 'fold', increasing the size of the contact patch and therefore providing better grip on acceleration. Tyre pressures are important here. If pressure is too high, the tyre cannot deform and the contact patch will overheat. If pressure is too low, the sidewall will move around too much and the whole tyre will again overheat. It's all a fine line between deformation and pressures. Of course, this is also affected by the rider and the way he uses the throttle. Someone with aggressive throttle control will need a little more tyre pressure than someone with a more progressive roll-on.

Lean angle is the biggest restriction to your acceleration plan. See how the riders are looking to get the bike upright as soon as possible to get the most acceleration. The longer you have the bike on its side, the harder it is to really drive off the corner. Spiking the throttle at the end of the turn is also not a good plan as it asks too much of the tyre; at best you lose drive because the wheel spins too much, at worst the tyre will give up the ghost and highside you.

As can be seen below, a rear tyre has huge demands placed on it – but not as much as a front tyre. The most severely worn area, near the wheel rim, has to cope with cornering forces as well as acceleration. Wear decreases towards the middle of the tyre, which only has to handle acceleration as cornering forces decrease when the bike is more upright.

The real art of riding a bike fast around a corner has to come from the skill of acceleration. Bikes, as we all know, make any supercar look stupid when it comes to getting out of corners and off down the straights. This is why most cars get thrashed on a race track by a standard road bike. Cars have better brakes and more grip but they just weigh too much and cannot get out of a corner fast enough to beat a bike.

But – and it's a big but – we have to take care as we don't have four wheels to support us in the corner. What we have are two tyres that are already up to their necks in keeping the bike from falling due to the cornering forces they have to cope with. Add to this some acceleration and the job for the tyre becomes even harder.

"If you have very much horsepower," says Valentino Rossi, "you need to put more tyre on the ground for when you open the throttle. I didn't really do this so much in 125s but I started using the technique a lot in 250s. And the more power you have, the more important it becomes, so I use this very much in 500s and also in MotoGP."

This is why motorcycle tyres have more technology in them and their manufacturing processes are more complicated than even the grippiest car tyre. It's the job of the tyre to provide enough grip to hold you on the track and allow you to accelerate as hard as possible out of the corner.

"It's important to have good throttle control," says 250 rider Chaz Davies. "That means having a good connection between your wrist and brain, and a good feeling for how close to the limit of traction you are when you can feel the rear tyre moving. There's a fine line between being too aggressive and not aggressive enough."

Acceleration sense is the foundation skill of cornering a bike. Leave it too long before you open the throttle and you run the risk of losing grip from the front end, never a nice option as front end losses are very hard to save (and you can forget saving it on your knee slider as this is more luck than a valid skill). Conversely, open the throttle too soon and you can lose the rear if you're carrying too much lean angle.

In both cases it's the transfer of the bike's weight that creates the problem. Too much on the front tyre and it will let go, and – just as bad – too little on the rear tyre and it will also let go. Of course, this also works the other way round: too little on the front and it will wash out, and too much on the rear – depending on lean angle – and it will slide as well.

Add to this the 'three stages of acceleration'

Because Chris Vermeulen is sitting close to the tank of his bike, his throttle hand and wrist are put in a difficult position for rolling on. If he moved back slightly, the roll-on would be smoother as his wrist and forearm wouldn't be so cramped. However, with over 200bhp you want to be ready to deal with the hard drive on the exit of the turn, and being over the front of your bike is definitely the place to be as the power is dialled in hard.

"WHEN RACING A MOTORCYCLE THERE SHOULDN'T BE ANYWHERE ON THE TRACK WHERE YOU AREN'T EITHER BRAKING OR ON THE THROTTLE. FROM THE MOMENT I LET THE BRAKE OFF I HAVE SOME THROTTLE TO KEEP THE BIKE STABLE AND THEN ACCELERATE AS HARD AND AS SOON AS I CAN."

CHRIS VERMEULEN

There's a fine line between drive and slide. While sliding has its place when you're trying to get out of a corner as quickly as possible, generally the less slide you have the better – less slide means more drive. Here Nicky Hayden can be seen balancing that fine line. Traction control has helped in this situation, but too much traction control will restrict acceleration – so it's still the job of the rider to play with the throttle and determine how much or how little of it is required.

we have to use in the corner and we can see why this becomes such a fine line between disaster and success.

"When racing a motorcycle," says Chris Vermeulen, "there shouldn't be anywhere on the track where you aren't either braking or on the throttle – there shouldn't be any period in between. From the moment I let the front brake off I have some throttle to keep the bike stable and then accelerate as hard and as soon as I can."

The first of the three types of acceleration is deceleration as you approach a corner. You could call this 'backwards' acceleration. The bike is slowing down. Weight transfers to the front and compresses the front forks, shortening the trail of the bike – as well as the wheelbase – and allowing it to turn more easily into the bend.

Nicky Hayden takes this a stage further. "I like to do most of my braking straight up and down. I really try not to coast on any corner. But at somewhere like Turn Two at Jerez, where it's really easy to run wide and it's downhill, I drag the front brake for a long, long time just to keep the bike turning. I'm not really slowing down, you know, just trying to keep weight on the front. I don't really need the front brake to slow down but just to get it in there and to get the bike to turn."

However, carry this too far into the corner and you risk the front tyre giving up the ghost and you finding yourself eating gravel – one reason why trail braking is fraught with hazards but a natural skill that GP riders use.

Once we're in the corner, we then move on to stage two: stabilising throttle. Now this is where we can make up time. This really is the key to getting those lap times to drop, where we can gain ground to overtake on the exit. This is when the bike is balanced and the tyres can cope. This is the moment when we have more grip and the ability to make use of it. And it's tiny.

Compared to how hard we can get on the throttle at the end of a corner, the throttle we use in the early and middle parts of a corner is when we can really show our skill levels.

"I'm sure there are some corners," says John Hopkins, "where the data would show I'm actually starting to open the throttle and I may still be on the brake. If you're not braking then you've got to be on the throttle – there should be no time in between. There are times racing a bike when you would like throttle control to be more gradual than it is, when you really have to brutalise the throttle and get on it harder than you'd like to. I like to have that little bit more horsepower at the beginning and then use a gradual roll on, just real light."

The closer the rider gets to the end of the corner, the more confident he becomes with the throttle. As you can see above, the throttle application of Toni Elias is going to be greater at this point than Casey Stoner behind him, Shinya Nakano behind him and John Hopkins right back in the middle of the turn. However, with traction control, it's highly likely that the first three riders have the throttle to the stop and are relying on the sophisticated engine management systems to give the right amount of drive and no slide.

As can be seen in the diagram below, the amount of throttle that can be used mid-corner is very little, but it's just as important as the full-throttle applications towards the end of the turn. Without some throttle in the early and middle parts of the corner the bike will mishandle, as it will have too much weight on the front of the bike and not enough on the rear. A bike with a mismatched weight balance in the corner won't hold its line and will give the rider more things to think about as well as restricting when he can apply acceleration. This would make the rider later on the throttle and therefore lead him to go from too little throttle to too much by the end of the corner. Having some throttle in the middle creates a lower demand on the tyre at the exit – ideal for maximum acceleration and tyre conservation.

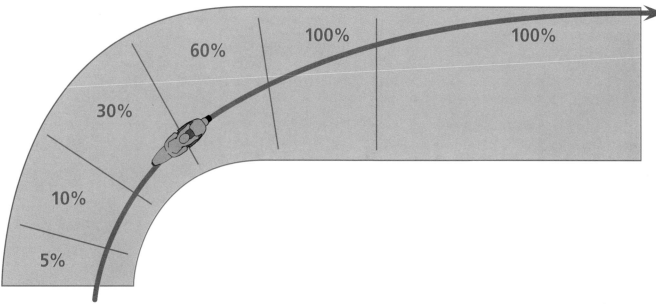

**1** In the first shot of this series showing James Ellison on his Dunlop-shod Tech 3 Yamaha accelerating through different corners, you can see how he's just gently using the throttle to keep the bike on his chosen line. If at this point he applied too much power he could highside and crash, but if he uses too little he could also crash with a lowside as a result of asking too much of the front tyre. The roll-on at this point is very little, but just as important as the drive on the exit (see the diagram on the previous page).

**2** James is off the front brake, having completed his braking action, and is now working on the application of the throttle to try to carry his corner entry speed into and through the rest of the turn. The sooner you can get back on the throttle, the quicker you can go through the turn. How well you can manage your speed at the entry of the corner will have a lasting effect on the remainder of the turn and your ability to accelerate at the end of the bend. If you go in too fast then you will be off the throttle for longer and therefore not accelerating out as well as if you went in a little slower. On a MotoGP bike, acceleration is the key to quicker lap times. On a 125, the same rules apply but you can get into the turn faster as the bike is lighter. The twist? It does not have the power to come out as fast...

**3** Looking for the exit of the turn as soon as you can is also a key factor in getting on the throttle harder. If you are looking at the front wheel then you have no space to drive the bike into and therefore will not be as brave on the exit as you should or could be. Acceleration is a useless tool if you have your eyes closed!

**4** Getting ready for the off. Now the end of the corner is in sight, drive and acceleration are going to get harder and harder. Getting the bike upright as soon as you can while keeping it on line will now be the key to acceleration. As we all know, if you pick the bike upright too soon then it will run to the outside of the corner. To overcome this, the rider can slide the rear of the bike, which will square off the line, and you don't run out of room. However, sliding is not driving – and not always the best plan of action.

A lot of riders complain that they cannot get on the gas hard enough because they overwhelm the tyre and slide rather than drive at the end of the turn. This is true even with a brand new slick on the rear. But the point here is that with more early and mid-corner throttle, the gains in speed are greater and the wear on the tyre and the rider is lower. I'm still amazed to see riders brake into a corner and then continue slowing down by leaving too big a gap between the brakes coming off and the throttle going back on.

Even to start with 0.5mm of throttle once your entry speed is set will help you carry this speed and gather more speed over the whole corner instead of trying to make it all back with a big handful at the exit of the turn.

In some corners this can mean using as little as 2-3mm of throttle cable to achieve this goal. Better, longer grip and more speed are the benefits and results of such action.

"I'm very progressive with the throttle," James Ellison says. "Whenever I get on the throttle I never get on it really hard. I just start opening it a little bit to start feeding the power on to about 10 or maybe 20 per cent of the throttle. Then, once I know there's going to be grip, BANG – and I go to full throttle. If you start coming out of a corner and start playing with the throttle, then you know you've come out on the wrong line. So you settle the bike with the first 10 to 20 per cent of it and then go to full throttle because the traction control will contain the slide. Normally on a bike

**5** Pin it! James now has the bike upright and the throttle to the stop. One of the bad habits you can take from road riding to the race track is not to get the throttle on the stop when the bike is upright. Getting to the stop as soon as possible with the bike completely upright can shave seconds off your lap times. Even on the shortest of straights between two corners, you can still roll to the stop. The key here is not to lose all the speed by then overbraking into the next corner!

**6** With the front wheel just kissing the surface, the bike is driving out of the corner as hard as is possible with no lift or wheelspin. See how James is now looking for the best possible body position to slip through the air and maximise speed before he hits the brakes and starts the whole process all over again. Of course, the next corner will be different in some way (camber, radius, surface) and will present a completely new series of acceleration challenges to overcome.

**4**

**5**

**6**

# The Good
WHEN IT ALL GOES RIGHT

Rossi on it. He has planned his acceleration well because he has the bike upright even though he's still on the exit kerbing. If you know where you want to be on the exit of a corner, then accelerating harder is less of an issue because you already know what the result will be. You start working ahead of the bike and this produces a flow, a rhythm that will allow you to get on the throttle harder.

You can see clearly here how Rossi has the confidence to run the bike right up to the grass and still have the front wheel just slightly off the ground!

# The Bad
WHEN IT ALL GOES WRONG

The pressure is on! When you have another rider sitting right behind you, you can hear them close to you in the corner. Of course, you want to stay in front so the pressure to get on the gas a little harder and a little sooner becomes even more of a challenge.

The result could be loss of drive through too much spin or in this case, with Casey Stoner, a huge wheelie on the exit of the turn, causing loss of acceleration. He's moving his body over the front of the bike to try to keep it down – much more preferable to closing the throttle!

# The Ugly
FAST, BUT...

Aaron Yates getting a Suzuki all out of shape and sideways during winter testing at Sepang in 2004. In fairness, this would be a little bit of playtime and letting down of hair! However, if this was a race then it wouldn't be effective, even if it looks spectacular: the bike won't exit the corner fast because of the sheer amount of spinning of the rear tyre.

An interesting point is the rider's body position: this tells us that he got to the end of the turn and just pinned it, with no real attempt to feed in the power – he must have been showing off for the camera!

without traction control, I would start to play with the throttle to try and find grip – but with a MotoGP bike you don't need to."

Nevertheless, Colin Edwards points out: "With the traction control it really helps late in the race when you've got no traction. You're still playing with the throttle a little bit. Traction control is different; it's not like that you have in a car where you can just get it on."

Once you get to the exit of the corner, you can start the 'drive' phase. This is when you really start to get on it – and hard. It's the moment when you feel you have the grip to get away with more gas. It's the moment when you start to bring the bike more upright, when you begin to feel you have enough space in front of you to allow such behaviour. It's the point you start to feel confident again.

Even now you'll still have hurdles to overcome. If you use too much acceleration too soon, the bike will run wide on the exit and you'll have to shut off to get back on line – never the choice of champions that one. In fact, MotoGP riders, with all that power under their right hand, are more likely to add even more throttle when faced with running wide. The purpose is to get the back end to slide out – which will bring the bike around and point it back in the right direction.

"A lot of riders spin it up right away coming off the apex and then pick it up and drive away," says John Hopkins. "But I don't really like spinning unless I need to. If I'm coming out of a corner and I'm running wide, I'd like to have that assurance that I can get on it a bit harder just to spin it and straighten it out a little more."

It's a tough one to master and you'll need the confidence of Rossi to do it. I've seen him, Haga and other top riders do exactly this when faced with trouble. The age-old racer's adage is, "If in doubt - pin it!" Or as the late, great Paris-Dakar rider John Deacon used to say in answer to all my off-roading and enduro problems I asked him about, "Pinned in Thurd". God Bless Ya, Deacs.

The other issue we face with exit acceleration is drive versus wheelies. I have to admit to finding it really cool to exit a turn with the front

Nicky Hayden driving and spinning so hard that the rear tyre is actually smoking. With this much spin you can see that the tyre has lost some traction as the rear of the bike is drifting to the outside of the corner. This is predictable because the bike still has some lean angle to the inside of the corner. The throttle looks like it's on the stop but Hayden will be making fine and subtle adjustments to get the end result – good acceleration.

Accelerating with extreme leans takes a steady and accurate throttle hand. If at this point you go for too much you'll be in trouble. Too little will also have the same effect. Look at the tyre and you can see how it's reacting to the application of the throttle – the contact has grown to help cope with the demands of cornering and acceleration. And bear in mind that a MotoGP bike has so much horsepower that the construction of the carcass will be very stiff, yet still it deforms! In this shot we know the rider is on the throttle because the chain is tight at the top and loose at the bottom – a sure sign of acceleration. How much throttle can be applied will be down to bike set-up, tyre choice and rider ability.

wheel in the air, but it's not going to make your lap times quicker. But it'll look cooler.

With the front wheel in the air, all of that power you've been applying has been wasted. That precious power has been used to lift the front of the bike, the wheel, the forks, the engine, the frame and you into the air. Imagine the weight of all those components, imagine grabbing the front wheel and lifting the whole bike by hand. Now think of the amount of power you could have been using to drive the bike forwards instead of skywards and you can see why it's not going to gain you those vital tenths of a second off your lap times. Had I realised this each time I wheelied over the Mountain at Cadwell Park waving to the crowd and not putting it down until the clubhouse, I might have got better lap times – but less applause!

"For sure, throttle control is the most important part of riding a bike," advises Rossi, wisely. "It's difficult with a big bike, like a MotoGP bike or big streetbike, because you can spin the rear tyre even in the dry. The only way to learn throttle control is experience, riding as many bikes as possible in as many conditions as possible. A few years ago I made some training with a motocross bike with enduro tyres on tarmac, just to slide easy and to understand the slide. I think the dirt is the best place to start this training.

"But basically you need to make many kilometres because you need to understand the power delivery of the bike. When you understand how and when the power arrives, it becomes more easy with the throttle. When I'm racing, I slide because in the middle of the corner I'm on the edge of the tyre. If you open the throttle when you don't have enough tyre on the ground you can start to spin and from that point you control the slide with the throttle. It's better to stay constant with the throttle, don't open, then shut when you get the slide, then open again because the bike becomes unstable. You need to feel the bike and stay with the throttle."

Getting the bike through the gearbox as quickly and smoothly as possible should be one of your riding goals. Most full-on race bikes have a quick-shifter but for track days and even in a race you need to know how to quick-shift yourself in case it packs up! At those times, when we're riding to high degrees of excitement, shifting quickly is just as important as planning how we're going to tackle the rapidly approaching bend. After all, if you have to back off, close the throttle, pull in the clutch, shift, let out the clutch and try and match the engine revs, you can become distracted and have your attention drawn away from the next turn, from braking or from any of the visual skills you need to go fast.

The misconceptions some riders have of the clutchless shift are interesting. The most common is that it'll destroy your gearbox. That's just not true, provided that you have a good technique and that your chain is adjusted correctly – not too tight and, most importantly, not too loose.

Certain classes of race bikes are allowed to use quick-shifters. These devices allow a rider to simply tap the gear lever with the throttle pinned to the stop to change gear. However, Mick Doohan once tested his Honda NSR500 with the quick-shifter disconnected and it only made 0.03 of a second's difference per lap. This means we have a new tool to master without the need for fancy electronics – at this stage – because 0.03 of a second is a lot in MotoGP terms.

The smooth clutchless shift is all down to your throttle application. Wind the throttle closed and then open and the bike will snatch as the gearbox and final drive chain go slack and then snap back when the power is reapplied.

Speed-shifting is a little smoother but it can ruin your bike's clutch! A speed-shift is when the rider keeps pressure on the gear lever and then stokes the clutch lever to allow the next gear selection to take place. The clutch then slips to catch up with the engine's increased revs, an effect of the clutch slipping.

The clutchless shift is simple to perform but will take some practice to get just right. And it's a technique that you should only use on your way up the 'box. Try and use it going down the 'box and you will struggle as the difference in engine revs and road speed is too great.

Here's how to do it. Drive through the revs until you get to the point where you want to shift up. Get your foot ready to move the gear lever. Now back off the throttle slightly, enough to stop acceleration but not so much that you start to decrease speed. Now shift and the gear will slot into place smoothly. And then get straight back on the gas.

The signs that your timing is off are quite simple. Close the throttle too much and the bike will snap and lurch into gear. Don't back off enough and you'll find it difficult to select the next gear.

Rossi looks even more deeply into it: "If I need to decide between a lower gear or a higher gear, I always go for the longer gear. It's better to be in a slightly taller gear than a slightly lower gear. The important thing with the choice of gear is that you need to stay where the engine has the best torque, not before and not after."

So the art of acceleration is one of timing and understanding the three component parts needed for each section of the corner. However, the golden rule is the sooner we can get the throttle

open, even if it's a matter of a metre earlier, the sooner we start to work with the bike and to achieve our goal of getting out of the corner as quickly as possible in the best possible shape – not out of shape.

Valentino Rossi having fun with acceleration. A small power wheelie out of a turn is just as good a crowd-pleaser as a long, near-vertical, one-handed wheelie. How do we know Rossi's having a bit of fun? He isn't behind the fairing with the throttle pinned!

Nicky Hayden taking the chequered flag at Losail in Qatar. Like an Olympic runner, a racer won't just coast over the line, even at the tail of the field. Keeping the bike pinned over the line could be all that's needed to get vital points. Head down, ass up and throttle open to the very stop – and then some more!

## HOW TO GET THE BEST TOP SPEED

It used to be a wonder to me when I saw the top speeds of bikes in road tests in the press. How did they always manage to achieve such a huge top speed? It was only when I began speed testing myself that the answer became apparent. How you position your body can have a massive effect on how fast you can get your bike to go. Even a small difference in body position can affect a bike's potential top speed by 5mph. MotoGP racers know this very well and are down behind the screen as soon as they can get out of a corner.

But first things first – you need a long piece of tarmac before you can even think about top speed potential. On the MotoGP trail, the straights at Losail, Catalunya, Valencia, Jerez, Shanghai and Mugello are the sorts of places where the riders are looking to get the best top speed figure.

To get to a bike's ultimate speed, the first thing you have to do is relax your grip on the handlebars to make the bike as stable as possible. The last thing you need at high speed is a tank slapper caused by hanging on with a death grip.

Now you're relaxed, bend your head forward and right behind the screen, getting so low that your chin should be resting on the fuel tank. This helps the airflow over the front part of the bike and this alone will give you good terminal velocity. However, if you want those last few mph, you'll need to move your bum back in the seat or onto the speed hump to create a more streamlined silhouette, allowing a smoother airflow as the wind leaves the back of the bike. Too much turbulence at the tail end will destroy your slippery shape and slow you down.

Finally, when the time comes to slow down, start braking BEFORE you sit up. Getting upright into a 210mph wind will certainly slow you down as you'll be acting like a huge sail, but you'll also act as a wing and weight will be lifted off the front of the bike – which can make it VERY unstable.

Olivier Jacque in a full-on racing crouch to get the best top speed from his Kawasaki MotoGP bike. This picture clearly shows why sports bikes have a recess in the fuel tank or airbox cover to allow the rider to get right down low and behind the screen of the bike, to reduce wind resistance. Olivier is right back on the seat to help the airflow over his body and to smooth the airflow as it detaches from the rear of the bike.

# BRAKING

## Perfecting your efforts to be the last of the late-brakers

In this shot Valentino Rossi's in much better shape for the start of the corner. His bike's more stable because the rear wheel is on the ground. He's braking just as hard as Alex Barros, but look at his left leg: you can see he's more securely locked into the bike, which is allowing him to keep his weight off his arms to a better degree than Barros. This alone can be the key to keeping the back wheel on the floor.

With the rear wheel in the air, the bike becomes more unstable and harder to keep under control on the entry to the turn. This shot also shows how hard you can brake. Greater forces are generated under braking than under acceleration – even on a 250bhp MotoGP bike!

Carbon brakes allow the rider to brake much later and harder than steel discs. They're also lighter, helping the unsprung weight of the bike. This is an important factor at the front end as it allows the bike to turn in more easily. For the rider the carbon brakes have a 'lag' between the first application of the brake lever and the reaction from the brakes as the carbon heats up. This delay needs to be allowed for in the rider's braking plan for the corner.

It's alleged that the only reason Valentino Rossi drives rally cars is to perfect his late-braking techniques. This makes sense. There's little traction in a rally car but braking forces are high, so it's possible the skill transfers.

Braking on track isn't the art of slowing down, as most people think. Braking is another tool for you to use to go faster, even though the sole purpose of brakes is to reduce speed.

Sound contradictory? Good! It means we've got you thinking. Brakes on a track are there to help you achieve the highest possible corner entry speed for your line and throttle-control plan. Yes, this will mean slowing down, but not too much – and not too little. You want to slow down just enough to get the bike into the first part of the corner at the right speed. How you do this is open to debate as this is one of the more controversial aspects of riding a bike on a race track.

There are some riders who use both the front and rear brakes, others who only use the front. Some riders trail brake (ie, they hold the brake on as they turn the bike in) but others don't – although most GP riders take advantage of the grip they have and the lightness of the bikes in order to carry braking all the way into the corner.

"I'm quite aggressive on the brakes," says Chaz Davies. "I tend to bang them on quite sharply at the first moment of braking, unless it's wet – in that case I'm more progressive, starting soft and getting harder."

While the sole purpose of braking is to slow down your bike to a suitable entry speed, how you brake can and does have a huge effect on your bike's balance and suspension.

"I always brake very much with the front, road or track," comments Valentino Rossi. "I would say I use 80 per cent the front and 20 per cent the rear. Really, you only stop the bike with the front brake. You use the rear just a little, to keep the bike stable. The difference between the track and the road is this – on the track you can use the front brake all the way into the corner."

Grabbing at the lever, being snatchy with it or using it as an on/off switch will make your bike unstable. If this occurs as you're entering a corner, the suspension will have little or no

time to settle before it has to deal with cornering forces. This instability can cause a loss in traction from the front as the tyre tries to make up for the things the suspension can't do as it tries to settle.

What we need to look at here isn't emergency braking, but braking to set you and your bike up for a corner in the best possible way.

As you brake, you compress the front suspension and unload the rear because the weight of the bike transfers to the front as it slows down. If you were now to release the lever sharply before you turn, the suspension will spring back as quickly as possible and then compress again as you start to move through the corner, making the bike seesaw into the first part of the turn. If, instead, you ease off the lever gently as you turn – or slightly before you turn – the suspension will move to its required point more progressively and then be settled (not moving), ready for

Loris Capirossi setting his speed for the approaching corner. Look at his body position: his hips are right up to the back of the tank, allowing some of the braking forces on his arms to be reduced. However, he'll need to move back in the seat if he's to hang off the bike effectively through the corner. You can also see that there's still travel available in the front forks, showing that Capirossi could brake harder if he needed to. It also shows how progressive he is with the right-hand lever...

100%

LEVER PRESSURE

FRONT BRAKE
REAR BRAKE

STRAIGHT
INTO CORNER

ENTRY OF CORNER POSITION
ON TRACK

CORNER
APEX

**Braking on track is the art of setting your speed for the corner. Most of your slowing down should be done with the bike upright, but trailing the brake into the corner and in some cases all the way up to the apex is a perfectly valid – if sometimes risky – technique in a racing situation. Use of the rear brake is tiny in comparison, and can only be done effectively on left-handers – otherwise your foot gets in the way of the ground! A thumb brake, like that used by Mick Doohan, overcomes this. However, on a 250bhp MotoGP bike there's a lot of engine braking that can be used. All MotoGP riders agree on one thing: the rear brake isn't used for slowing down...**

the turn and associated cornering forces.

If it were represented as a graph, your use of the brake should trace a line like the back of a brontosaurus. Initially you apply the brake gently, but with enough pressure to compress the suspension. When the compressed suspension becomes stable, you apply the brakes harder. Then, as you get to the point where you want to let go, you gently release the pressure.

This gentle-hard-gentle approach to braking not only allows you to brake harder through the period when you need to scrub off the most speed, but also – with accurate and softer pressure on the lever – really refines your corner entry speed as you haven't got all those braking forces trying to cloud your judgement of your speed. Rushing up to the turn with full and aggressive braking tends to overload you with deceleration forces, so that you have a masked and less accurate ability to tell if your entry speed will be right. Remember, soft-hard-soft...as the actress said to the bishop.

So, braking on the race track becomes the art of setting your entry speed for a corner. It isn't a device used to stop you as on the road, but a tool used only to slow you down. That's the biggest difference between road and track riding. It's rare that you'll want to come to a complete stop on the track. Off the track maybe, but there'll be

other issues to deal with in that scenario...

Use of the brakes seems to be the one area where racers just cannot agree. This is mainly down to the fact that on a bike there are two sets of the things. Differences of opinion arise mainly over the use of the rear brake and whether it's a useful tool or just another distraction as you reach one of a motorcycle racer's busiest moments – the entry to a corner.

If we examine how a bike is designed and what happens under braking, maybe we can decide for ourselves what use the rear brake has. My own view is that a rear brake is good for skidding and SuperMotos, but otherwise it's just an ornament!

John Hopkins agrees: "I hardly ever use the rear brake. To be honest it should be painted red and have the words 'In Case Of Emergency Only' printed on it. If I go off in the gravel, I'll use it – but really that's all. Because I just don't use the rear brake, we have the thinnest, lightest disc we can use. Especially with the four-stroke, it's just not appropriate."

However, if we look at Nicky Hayden's bike we can clearly see that he uses the rear brake rather more often. In fact, the larger-than-normal rear disc on his Honda RCV211 is alleged to come from a 250, and his preference for it comes from his dirt-tracking background.

"People look at my bike," says Nicky, "and

## TWO RIDERS, SAME TEAM, DIFFERENT REAR BRAKE

Nicky Hayden's Repsol Honda RCV211. Nicky uses the rear brake more than his team-mate as he has a larger rear disc as well as a larger rear brake caliper to allow the disc to run cooler. His specification goes back to his dirt-racing days in the USA, where he learned to race on bikes without a front brake!

Dani Pedrosa's Repsol Honda RCV211. Dani's bike has a much smaller disc and caliper than Hayden's. Because use of the rear brake figures less in Pedrosa's braking plan for the corner, less heat is generated in his bike's rear disc. This comes from Dani's progression through the ranks of 125GP and 250GP, where the front brakes are more effective for setting speed as there's little engine braking on a two-stroke.

think I use it so much because it's big, but it's that big to stop it getting hot. It's got no more power than a normal disc on a normal bike. I grew up dirt-tracking so the rear brake was your only option – that or the kill switch. I use it for a lot more than braking: I use it to control a wheelie and to steady the bike when changing direction. I use the front brake a lot as I like to do most of my braking straight up and down."

Here's another point of view, from Chaz Davies: "I use the rear brake. Sometimes I use it when braking in a straight line if the rear is a bit loose on the brakes, to try and keep it in line. But mainly I use it on corner entry as far as mid-corner to keep the bike in towards the apex and to help the bike turn in."

But let us first look at some hard facts. Race bikes have two discs up front with massive calipers to get the bulk of the work done. This is the same on nearly all road bikes too – certainly sports bikes and sports tourers. The front discs on a race bike are generally 320mm in diameter to help cope with the heat generated when slowing down. In addition, carbon discs offer even more braking power as well as being lighter. But no MotoGP teams use carbon for the rear disc, so we can only conclude that the rear brake isn't really used much for slowing down. However, on a 125 it seems that there's more to it.

"Using the rear brake makes a 125 feel more stable," says 2005 125 World Champion Thomas Lüthi. "Also on a 125 you use as much engine braking as you can, but there's not much of this so the rear brake helps. I also carry the rear brake for a long time into the corner, but not so hard."

The rear disc of a MotoGP bike is much smaller, as little as 245mm, and it's gripped by a single-piston caliper in most cases. But even with this tiny disc on the rear, it's frightening how easily you can lock up the rear wheel. When you add in the fact that you're wearing a bulky race boot, you can see how difficult it is to achieve refinement in your use of the rear brake.

"I use the rear brake a bit more in left-handers to try and slow the bike and pull it in," points out Chaz Davies. "In right-handers it's a little

**BRAKING**
Under braking, the weight of the bike and rider is thrown forwards and the bike pivots over the front wheel. Having your arms almost straight, as seen here, can allow the rear wheel to lift from the track, making the bike less stable.

**FLAT OUT**
The rider's weight is almost equal over both wheel axles as he has the throttle to the stop. Nevertheless, he's still trying to keep some weight over the front end – look where his ass is in comparison to the bum stop on the tailpiece.

100%            0%            50%
WEIGHT DISTRIBUTION

more tricky getting the foot to the rear brake."

One thing nearly all top riders agree on is that use of the rear brake can help to tighten your line mid-corner. Bear in mind, though, that this is on a MotoGP bike with the world's stickiest slick tyres. I'm not so sure it would work as well at a track day, on a production bike with track day or Supersport tyres.

All this just goes to show how much spare attention a world-class racer has. There's a lot to think about on the entry to any corner as it's the busiest part of any turn – Keith Code has identified 46 points. The more things you add during the entry, the harder it becomes. Couple this with the fact that racers look to compress their braking space into as short a distance as possible (and therefore the braking forces acting on them will be as fierce as they can possibly be), then it's an amazing skill to be able to use that foot pressure with subtlety into the corner.

Luckily, the feel we have on the front brake lever is much more refined and we can use just one finger on a MotoGP bike to create the most amazing amount of deceleration.

But all that front-end braking potential is limited by the small dimensions of the front tyre (typically 120 section). At the rear the sheer size of the tyre (180 or 190 section) offers incredible grip, but it's still easy to lock up – this is commonly

seen at track days. So we're left with a bit of a quandary: at the front there's a small tyre but huge braking power; and at the rear there's a massive tyre but limited braking power. However, as we all know and have felt, a rear-wheel slide is a damned sight easier to control and recover from than a front-wheel slide.

So, what's the goal when braking on a race track? The aim is to set your speed in the shortest possible distance so that you can keep the throttle wide open for longer on the straights. For example, if you start braking at the 200-metre board from 120mph to a corner-entry speed of 60mph, you'd scrub off 60mph in 200 metres. If you can leave your braking for a further 50 metres, you gain an extra 50 metres at 120mph – a few vital tenths of a second off your lap times.

However, if you leave your braking later, the forces you generate get greater. Later equals greater – pure and simple. Later braking also compresses the time available for decision-making: assessing how much grip you have from the front; judging whether the front will lock; assessing the corner; deciding where you're going to go next (hopefully into the corner and not straight on); working out whether you're setting your speed correctly (not too high or not too low); observing whether you're going to get passed by another rider or pass someone yourself; and, most

Steel disc brakes (facing page) offer more feel when you first apply pressure to the brake lever, as steel heats up almost immediately. Because of this, steel discs are often used by top race teams in wet weather. One downside of steel, however, is that it retains heat for longer, so pad material is important to ensure that the brakes don't overheat in a race.

**ACCELERATION**
Weight transfers to the rear of the bike under acceleration, forcing the rear tyre into the ground. The rider gets his weight as far forward as possible to try to keep the front wheel on the floor.

50%          20%          80%

THE INTRODUCTION OF SLIPPER CLUTCHES MEANS A MOTOGP RIDER NO LONGER NEEDS TO BLIP THE THROTTLE FOR SMOOTH DOWNSHIFTS UNDER BRAKING, THUS FREEING UP ADDITIONAL FINGERS TO BRAKE WITH (GIVING MORE FEEL) FOR THE IMPORTANT JOB OF ACCURATELY ADJUSTING THE ENTRY SPEED FOR THE CORNER.

of all, if you'll be able to hang on to the bike while the back end tries to lift off the ground as you apply more brake while fast running out of room!

Late braking is where a lot of first-timers to the track tend to let themselves down. Late braking can be viewed as the prelude to a crash! When you ride on the road, the rule for braking is one of survival and the crucial goal, in most cases, is to get as much speed off as quickly as possible until you reach a complete stop. This requires that you brake harder and harder as the bike slows, thus decreasing your stopping distance and reducing the chance of locking the front wheel through more progressive use of the brake lever.

But the aim for track riding is to set your speed. Of course, this requires that you reduce your speed – but to a set speed, not to a stop.

Braking, therefore, can be approached differently on the track depending on where in the corner – or on the way into it – you want your speed set by.

Generally we have to look at how the bike can react to your input on the lever. If you're rough or aggressive with it, then the bike will react accordingly. The reverse applies if you're smooth with the lever.

Keeping the bike under control and not out of shape on the way into the turn allows you to devote more attention to the job in hand, to get in there as fast as possible. The more your bike is out of shape, the more of your attention it will take to keep it under control.

Under braking there's a bigger transfer of weight, rear to front, than at just about any other time. This affects the front suspension radically and can cause the bike to get unwieldy, depending on how quickly that transfer takes place. To help the bike remain under control, we need to look at braking a little first, then hard – no, make that really *hard* – to scrub as much speed as possible, and then refining our corner entry speed with a lessening brake the closer we get to the corner.

As an aside, there was a time when Johnny Haynes, the UK's Chief Riding Coach at the California Superbike School, was having problems with his bike under braking. When educated on this technique, he found the bike was under better control and for most turns he also had to move his braking marker further down the track.

The initial gentle squeeze allows the front suspension to start compressing progressively. Once you brake hard, the dive resulting from the extra pressure takes less fork travel as the job has already been started. Then as you gradually release the pressure the forks slowly return, instead of being unloaded suddenly as you snap the lever off. This gives more grip at the turn entry as the forks haven't completely unloaded. And it's

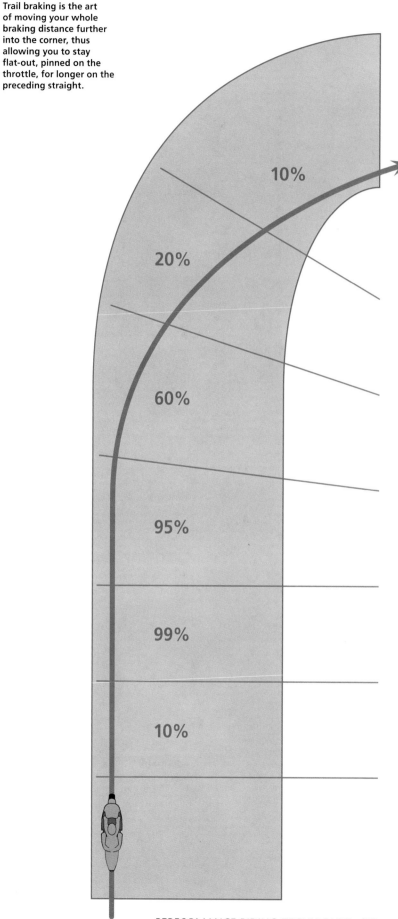

Trail braking is the art of moving your whole braking distance further into the corner, thus allowing you to stay flat-out, pinned on the throttle, for longer on the preceding straight.

**1** Valentino Rossi demonstrates how, with some bend in the arms, you can make the transfer of weight go through the bike rather than to the front of the bike.

**2** Rossi's knee is out ready for the corner. However, would it be more useful to leave it in to help take the braking forces? It's not even close to dragging on the floor yet.

**3** Notice that Rossi is using a little bit of rear brake in an attempt to keep the bike more balanced.

**4** Head up and gauging his entry speed, the next stage will be to look into the corner to make a plan for when to release the brakes and where to apex. How and when you get off the brakes is just as important as when you start to apply them.

this that will also allow you to trail brake. If you were to pitch the bike in on full brakes and then sharply release them, the front of the bike would react and could slide through lack of weight. The front tyre does have a job to do in the corners!

Let's move on to the final part of the braking puzzle: you, the rider. What you do with your upper body when braking greatly affects the way the bike feels and how you feel.

The first aspect to discuss is 'forearm pump'. Here are some illuminating comments from top riders in response to being asked whether they've ever suffered from it.

John Hopkins: "Never, because I grew up on Motocross. I've never ever suffered from it on a street bike or road race bike."

James Ellison: "Never on the track. Only on Motocrossers."

Chris Vermeulen: "I've had it once or twice, but that's all. I had it once on a FireBlade at Knockhill and once at Cadwell Park – funny places. I guess I wasn't as comfortable riding and a little tense."

The main cause of 'forearm pump' is gripping the handlebars too tightly, particularly under braking, as a result of trying to brace your upper body against the forces you're creating.

Two problems are created. The first is the pump itself, and the second is the way your bike's

stability is affected: your bike is more likely to lose grip on the front and the back can come up off the floor under braking.

When your arms are locked out like broomsticks to take the braking forces, all your upper body weight is immediately transferred to the handlebars. This adds weight to the compression of the forks and lightens the load on the rear of the bike, causing it to lift. In this situation your upper body weight is also trying to move you over the handlebars, making a driving force that wants to throw you over the front – and giving a pivot point in front of the bike.

Now, if you can take the braking forces through another part of your body, then you'll discover two important points. Firstly, forearm pump will be reduced. Secondly, the bike will be more planted.

The key is to let your arms be as relaxed as possible while your legs grip the tank, so that most of the braking forces are taken through the tank instead of the handlebars. Remember that the bars are there as a means of control, not as a support for your upper body weight!

Thomas Lüthi, 2005 125GP World Champion, is a good example of a rider who uses his legs more than most. When he approaches a corner, he sets his inside leg in position to get his lean-angle indicator (his knee slider) on the floor and then he'll bring his leg in as he brakes and let it out as he turns the bike in. Excellent.

Many riders brace on the bars and look out of control – and that's because they are!

Here's a comment from Chris Vermeulen: "While I'm braking I use pressure on both the foot pegs to help take the braking forces and to get my weight into my thighs and the tank. My centre of gravity is lower too."

This should also tell you something about any gym work you may be considering...

## TRAIL BRAKING

Carrying front brake into a turn gives the tyre a lot more workload to cope with than under normal cornering. As well as trying to grip the road surface, the tyre is also having to cope with the forces generated by the brake and the increasing cornering forces, which are trying to push the tyre

to the outside of the turn. You can see a lot of excellent riders push this a little too far and end up lowsiding. There's less feedback from the front end as the suspension is compressed more than normal because of the braking forces.

The ideal is to do most, if not all, of your braking before you turn the bike as this carries the least risk of losing the front end. However, if you do carry some brake into a turn as the bike is leaning, then release it progressively as you approach the apex. This can be your greatest point of lean and therefore also the point of least traction, because the contact patches of the tyres are having to deal with cornering forces and braking forces at the same time – and the suspension is too compressed to help out much.

"I don't use trail braking on all corners," says 2005 125 World Champion Thomas Lüthi. "I tend

"YOU WANT TO RUN THE BIKE IN WITH AS MUCH SPEED AS POSSIBLE AND USE THE BRAKE TO CONTROL THE BIKE'S SPEED. OBVIOUSLY THE MORE LEAN ANGLE YOU'RE CARRYING THE LESS BRAKE YOU USE, BUT YOU'LL NEED TO LET GO OF THE BRAKE IN A DIFFERENT PLACE EVERY CORNER."
**CHRIS VERMEULEN**

# The Good
## WHEN IT ALL GOES RIGHT

Marco Melandri setting his speed. He's using the full width of the track at this point to make sure he can get the best possible braking distance into the turn. If he were further to the inside, then the line he'd have to use wouldn't be as effective for trailing the braking into the corner.

In spite of the slipper clutch that's fitted to his Honda, his fingers are still covering the clutch lever – no doubt an old habit from his 500, 250 and 125 two-stroke days. A two-stroke rider covers the clutch in case the engine seizes at any point, thus potentially saving a crash.

# The Bad
## WHEN IT ALL GOES WRONG

Even our riding gods get it wrong from time to time. Max Biaggi shows how much power there is under the right fingers as he tries to slow down in time so that he doesn't torpedo Loris Capirossi. Despite this extreme stopping manoeuvre, he didn't manage it and took them both off.

T-boning your fellow riders isn't something that's expected at the top level, but incidents are common in club racing, particularly in the first corner when a lot of places can be won or lost. Note that Biaggi is looking straight ahead at the imminent point of impact.

# The Ugly
## OFF THE TRACK

There's only so much room you have, and when it goes wrong the only chance you have is to let go of the brakes, sit the bike up, and run off the track in relative control. Sete Gibernau has done just that and is running towards the barriers at high speed, so now he has to work out how to slow down on the low-friction surface.

Both front and rear brakes are being used in an attempt to keep the bike upright and get back on track. Too much front now and the bike will crash, but conversely too much rear and it'll slide. The rider has more control over a rear slide, particularly at lower speeds.

to go on the brake at the braking point very hard and try to get off the brake as early as possible. As soon as I'm comfortable with my speed I want to get off the brake and on to the throttle as early as I can."

Trail braking is a high-risk way of riding and you'll see more lowsides (front-end losses) than highsides (rear-end losses) in GP riding. There's very little warning that the front is going to break away and the only cure is to get back to throttle to take weight off the overloaded front tyre.

"On GP bikes I'd say that 60 per cent of my braking is done with the bike leant over," comments John Hopkins. "It started with the 500s and has carried over to the four-strokes."

A point of thought for you before you try this. World-class riders run on slicks with the best grip in the world and they still lose the front – how do you think your road or track tyre would cope?

Chris Vermeulen gives his thoughts on this subject: "You want to run the bike in with as much speed as possible and use the brake to control the bike's speed. Obviously the more lean angle you're carrying the less brake you use, but you'll need to let go of the brake in a different place every corner."

And James Ellison's comments: "I use trail braking now. I didn't use to. I used to run into the corners off the brakes. But on MotoGP bikes the

point between getting off the brakes and on the gas is the time when the suspension is unloaded and that's when it chatters. I'd say I use it more in the slower corners, but not the fast ones."

## REAR WHEEL LOCK-UP WHEN SHIFTING DOWN AND BRAKING

Failing to match your engine revs to your speed when you downshift can cause the rear wheel to lock up, and it also does nothing for your rear shock, tyre and chain as the back of the bike jumps up and down in a frantic attempt to catch up!

Achieving a smooth downshift, particularly during braking, means increasing the engine revs as you change down through the gearbox. This will help the bike to slow down smoothly. This is why top road riders and racers only use one, two or three fingers on the front brake. With MotoGP bikes it's slightly different because the brakes are awesome, and most of the bikes now have slipper clutches.

The carbon front brakes also make a big difference, as James Ellison explains: "All the braking is done in the first 50 metres. But with carbons, when you grab the brake you don't think you're going to stop – at first there's nothing there. You have to get it into your head

As a race progresses, the front and rear tyres wear and their level of grip reduces. This makes trailing the brake even harder at the end of a race than at the beginning. Here we see Nicky Hayden exceeding the limit in the final part of the 2005 race at Valencia – note his braking fingers.

that the bike will actually stop." There's a slight lag with carbon brakes because they need some heat build-up to work effectively.

The problem with hard front braking comes when your attention switches from the brake to front tyre traction. The harder the front tyre digs in, the more of a worry losing the front becomes. If you were to brake a little earlier and have a precise idea of exactly where you want to set your speed, you'd be more accurate with your entry speed and have more attention left to deal with turning the bike into the corner. By braking later and harder, all you'll do is make a mistake on speed judgement and end up going into the first part of the turn too slowly, leaving you trying to make up the ground on the power – an idea of limited potential as you'll be leant over and have less traction as a result.

Be easy on yourself and have more time to set up the corner. What you lose in late braking you will more than make up in entry speed and an ability to get on the throttle sooner and harder, giving you more exit speed.

Even if you're a racer, the more gently you start and end your braking, the less your attention will be spent on making it easier to re-overtake the guy who has dived up the inside all out of shape and run in too hot. The only time this won't work is when the rider who has just

passed makes you stall on the throttle, thus making his mistake also yours. Give yourself more time and the rewards will be huge.

Start getting comfortable with using the thumb and spare fingers to control the throttle while using the front lever. This technique is valuable whether you're going to blip on the downshift or you're looking to get back into the throttle as soon as possible after braking.

When you start to brake and then go for a lower gear, make sure you blip the throttle before you release clutch so that the rear wheel doesn't have to try and make the engine spin faster to match its speed.

If the span width on your bike's lever can be adjusted, make any necessary adjustment so that the action of blipping doesn't interfere with the smoothness of your braking. If blipping the throttle makes your braking fingers roll on and off the lever, effectively pulsing the front brake, try using one less finger until you can blip and still brake progressively.

Mind you, on-board MotoGP footage reveals that Valentino Rossi sometimes uses four fingers when braking. This appears to be completely contrary to what we have seen over the past few decades from all types of professional riders – they have been using a combination of two fingers to brake. So what's going on?

**Thomas Lüthi clearly demonstrating use of both knees to lock into the fuel tank for better control of the bike under braking. When the bike is upright there's little or no point in sticking your knee into the wind. Use that knee to help reduce fatigue by having two points of contact with the bike rather than one.**

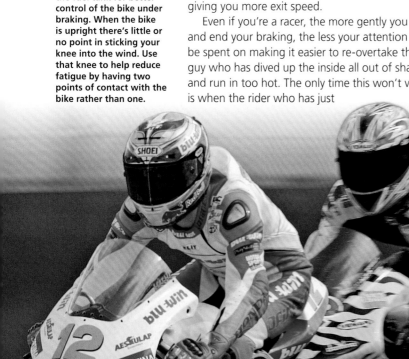

**1**

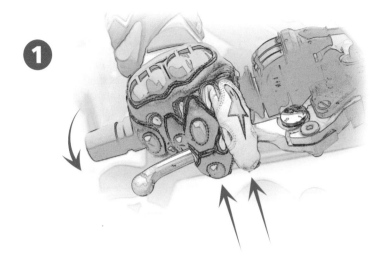

**2**

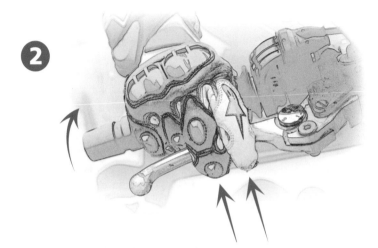

The correct procedure for down-shifting during braking should be:

■ **START BRAKING**
■ **CLUTCH IN**
■ **SELECT GEAR**
■ **BLIP THROTTLE**
■ **CLUTCH OUT**

**3**

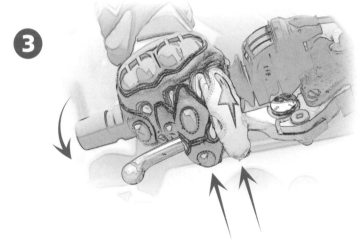

**1** Start braking and roll off the throttle. As you reach your downshifting point, squeeze the clutch lever and start to shift down.

**2** At the same time, blip the throttle, thus increasing the engine's rpm to match the lower gear ratio you've selected. Make sure your pressure on the brake lever remains consistent. If not, then reduce the number of fingers on the lever.

**3** Once engine revs have risen, release the clutch and close the throttle. Keeping the throttle even partly open will make the bike surge forward. The key here is to be as smooth and progressive as possible.

The reason we use two fingers for braking is to leave a couple of digits spare to be able to blip the throttle when changing down through the gearbox. This allows downshifts to be smoother, which in turn makes the bike more stable during deceleration on the approach to a corner.

However, when Rossi's shifting down through the box, you'll see that he doesn't bother with the blip thanks to his bike's slipper clutch – and that's a good job really as it's very, very difficult to blip with just your thumb on the throttle under heavy braking. The slipper clutch allows a rider to downshift without the need to match engine revs with rear wheel speed, as the transmission makes up for this lack of blipping by slipping the clutch to allow the wheel and engine speeds to match. It's another sign of how bike technology is helping riders to perform even better at these extreme levels.

But for those of us with 'ordinary' clutches (RSV-Rs, ZX6-RRs and a few others excepted), we'll still need a bit of blipping – which means a combination of two fingers on the front lever. What will they think of next? Launch control and electronic self-adjusting steering dampers?

## 'BACKING IT IN'

Using the rear brake to 'back it in' requires an extraordinary amount of concentration as the chances of locking up the rear wheel are very high indeed. In reality you should use engine braking to get the bulk of the job done, but some rear brake is needed to get the result – too much, though, and the back end will come round too far and result in a crash.

The reason for using the back brake at all is so that you can keep the rear wheel spinning more slowly than the front wheel. It's this factor that controls the slide and allows you to get the bike turned in and towards the apex of the corner. While feathering the rear you'll need to be hard on the front brakes too. After all, you're approaching a corner and need to set your speed. Hard on the front makes the weight of the bike transfer to the front, which is good as the back of the bike

lightens and therefore it becomes easier for you to make it slide.

So far so good: the bike is out of line as you enter the first part of the corner. Now comes the hard part. You need to start to turn the bike (remembering that the more you lean the less grip you have), release the pressure on the brake slowly enough for the tyre not to suddenly grip, and get on the power to maintain the slide and therefore the attitude of the bike, so that it's pointing up the track on the exit.

As you might have already worked out, this is easier to accomplish on left-handers than right-handers. With right-handers, you'll need to be able to get off the brake and into a knee-down position as or even before you turn the bike. This will be much easier if you have a thumb-operated rear brake because you can do it on both left-handers and right-handers. On top of all this, you still have the front brake to control, the throttle to apply; you need to be looking into the turn, spotting your reference points, setting your body position – and so on.

So it's easy to see why 'backing it in' is rarely seen in MotoGP and never in the 250 and 125 classes. It would add yet another dynamic to the whole melting pot of getting the bike into the turn. Sometimes, when the TV commentators start ranting on about a rider backing it in, all

the rider is doing is getting out of shape. I've often seen a racer approach a corner with the bike sideways only to straighten it up before actually turning into the corner. Backing it in is what you see in SuperMoto racing where the bike is sideways all the way to the apex and beyond. It's fast for SuperMoto because the tracks they use are much slower with tighter turns than in MotoGP racing. A SuperMoto rider is looking to deal with the compromises of the bike (it's an off roader!), the tyres (they're designed for 250s) and the track (a go-kart track normally). In MotoGP the bikes are designed to get into and out of corners as fast as possible, so the grip levels are higher and the bikes more dedicated to the job. As a result the 'backing it in' style rarely works out to be faster.

Having said all that, 'backing it in' is a good technique to learn as it provides a wonderful sense of traction – and, to be fair, it looks really cool when you do it. It's getting easier to do with slipper clutches as well, so we might as well take an advantage where and when we might need it. It's much better to have a tool in your bag to use once in a while than to find a time you need to do it and not know how. Certainly more and more MotoGP riders are looking towards SuperMotos for their fun and winter training as Motocross bikes these days.

**'Backing it in'** definitely works better in tighter and slower corners; it has little effect in long, fast, open sweepers. Here, however, we can see the risk of using this technique. Marco Melandri ended up crashing shortly after this shot was taken.

# CORNERING & STEERING

**This is where your
skill really matters**

Getting your bike into a corner quickly means turning the bike quickly – the quicker the better. Look at the position of Kawasaki rider Shinya Nakano compared with that of Sete Gibernau. Nakano will have as few as five bike lengths to get his bike from upright to the desired lean angle if he's going to get through the corner at his current speed. If he's travelling at 60mph at this point he'll cover 88 feet in one second or roughly 12 bike lengths. He'll have half a second to turn the bike in to the correct lean angle and line. Could you?

Getting a bike into and out of a corner is different for different riders, different circuits, different corners, different tyres and different bikes. A 125 rider will have a different plan from a MotoGP rider. A Kawasaki will be different from a Suzuki. A Dunlop-shod rider will have a different plan from a Michelin-shod rider. And so on.

A very good example of this is Simon Crafar, who set the outright lap record at Donington Park in 1998 riding a 500cc Yamaha two-stroke on Dunlop tyres. When he switched the following year to another tyre brand, he couldn't ride the same way and had a poor season.

Each rider's line will be based on the amount of front and rear grip he feels he has, how quickly he can turn the bike, how quickly the bike can turn, how good his brakes are, how good he is at braking, when he can apply the throttle, what his throttle plan is, and what he's looking at and when. But despite all this, racers want the best of all worlds. They want to go in fast and come out fast. Unfortunately, the laws of physics just don't allow this to happen. You can:

**1 GO IN FAST BUT COME OUT SLOW**

**2 GO IN SLOW BUT COME OUT FAST**

**3 GO IN SLOW AND COME OUT SLOW**

**4 GO IN FAST AND NOT COME OUT**

Points 1 and 2 are acceptable in different circumstances, but 3 and 4 simply aren't an option when you're trying to gain a place in a race or get further up the grid in qualifying.

### SQUARING IT OFF. WHAT'S THAT ALL ABOUT?

'Squaring it off' is a term often heard from top riders, but what does it really mean? Do we, as lesser riders or racers, need to do it, or do we have to wait until we reach the stratosphere of GP racing for it to be really understood? It's all about where you turn in and the resultant line. You have only two choices when it comes to starting a corner: you either turn early or you turn late. Yes, of course there are all the points between those extremes, but early or late are the only real decisions you have.

Turning later into the corner – squaring it off – is better, but it's smothered in riding fears, those things that we do without thought at the wrong time and in the wrong place, like sitting the bike up when we feel too fast at the apex of a turn.

Lean angle is ultimately a rider's enemy. The further you lean a bike over, the less traction you get as the cornering forces on the tyre increase. A bike leant over 10 degrees has less cornering force on the tyre than a bike leant over 50 degrees. The cornering force is always trying to push the tyre to the outside of the corner.

A rider can help by using his body weight. Getting his body weight to the inside of the bike will allow the rider to get the bike a little more upright while still maintaining the line. We all know that if you pick the bike up it wants to run wide, but the weight of the rider on the inside will counter this. It's subtle, as can be seen here with Makoto Tamada – the line of his spine is not parallel to the line of the bike.

"I try to turn the bike more when I miss the apex," says 2005 125cc World Champion Thomas Lüthi. "It's sliding on both tyres and I try to push the bike more to the inside line by leaning my body further into the corner."

It's much easier for us to turn early as this doesn't induce too much fear at the entry to the corner – the fear kicks in later when we discover we're running wide and out of track pretty damned quickly! But turning later, or squaring off the entry to the corner, has several advantages over the 'classic' line, where you turn early.

### EXAMPLE A – THE EARLY TURN

Turning in early, which is commonly done, makes the corner have the least radius possible. This line seems fine on the face of it and on paper it looks perfect, but under closer scrutiny it's not as good as it might be. It's based on an old riding technique from the '30s and '40s when bikes had skinny tyres and ineffective suspension, making it impossible to square off a corner. Because of these factors, this used to be the fastest way through a turn, but chassis technology and tyres have moved on.

Once a rider has seen the start of a corner and begins to turn the bike, it's the classic 'go where you look' reaction. This starts the lean angle, as a bike isn't turning unless it's leaning. The lean angle increases the further into the turn you go as you fight the centrifugal force pushing you to the outside. You're likely to carry your highest angle of lean in the middle of the corner. Carrying lots of lean means your traction is reduced, making it harder to get on the throttle to balance the bike: all the weight is on the front of the bike, making it feel unstable and unwilling to hold the line.

As you come into the corner your field of view is more restricted when you turn in early. You'll be less accurate with your line because you can't plan the later half of your line through the corner.

The end result is that you might go in more quickly by turning early, but you'll come out more slowly on a poorly predicted line that will run you wide on the exit – and create its own problems!

### EXAMPLE B – SQUARING OFF

By going into a corner later, you can counter many of the problems of the 'classic' line. For a start, you'll see more of the corner before you turn the bike, so you can be more accurate with your chosen line.

In the middle of the turn the bike will be more upright, so you'll have more grip. More grip means that you can get back to throttle sooner, making the bike accelerate earlier in the corner, giving more exit speed.

This technique will mean you have to come into the corner more slowly, but you'll get out on the other side a lot faster, on a predictable line and more likely to be in one piece because you haven't drifted wide, as this line gives you more room – not less – on the exit.

Also, if you can shorten the time between turning the bike in and getting back on the power, you'll have the best possible traction for your chosen angle of lean, and the suspension will work better because the bike will be better balanced, with slightly more weight to the rear.

Try it. Turn a little later into corners. Try just one bike length later on a corner you know well and see how much better it becomes.

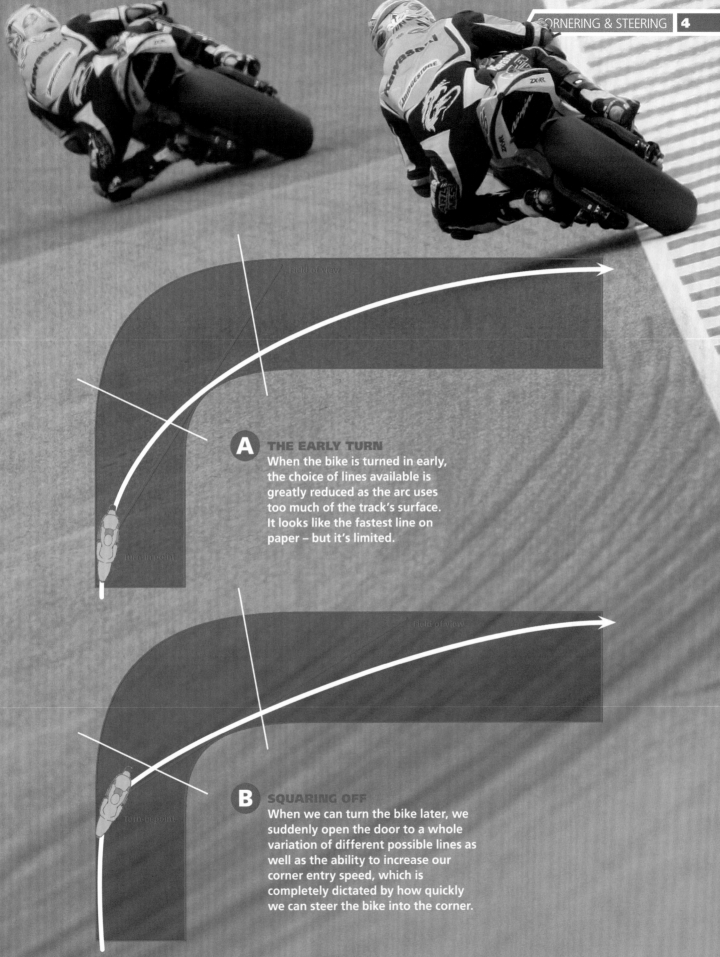

### A THE EARLY TURN

When the bike is turned in early, the choice of lines available is greatly reduced as the arc uses too much of the track's surface. It looks like the fastest line on paper – but it's limited.

### B SQUARING OFF

When we can turn the bike later, we suddenly open the door to a whole variation of different possible lines as well as the ability to increase our corner entry speed, which is completely dictated by how quickly we can steer the bike into the corner.

Chris Vermeulen getting his Suzuki to turn in – you can see the pressure on the outside foot peg. He's using the arch of his foot to make sure he has a good strong pivot point to steer from.

## CHARGING TURNS:
## BRAKING HARD AND LATE

The fastest riders are always the smoothest. While it's undoubtedly entertaining to see top racers getting out of shape, it's the smoother riders such as Valentino Rossi or Dani Pedrosa who win more of the races.

As Nicky Hayden says: "I like to keep working up to it and working up to it. One of the things we have on our bikes now is little lights; when you go through T1, T2, T3, if it's fastest you'll be given a little light. That's pretty cool."

When we make the decision to 'go faster', rather than work on more exit speed, a lot of the time our general mindset is to brake later and harder at the beginning of the turn – which starts overloading our senses and making our riding ragged and definitely slower. This is known as charging the turn: it's when we leave the braking so late that we devote all of our attention to slowing down and very little else, so we end up with a braking action that involves a sudden grab and sudden release of the right-hand lever, making the bike very unstable.

We also lock our arms out because we're braking hard and need to brace ourselves to avoid getting thrown over the front of the bike. However, we'll be able to brake harder, and get more feel and feedback from the bike, if we relax

our arms and use our legs to lock into the bike instead. As you approach a turn, get your body into position before you brake.

Your backside should be in place ready for the corner a long way before it's time to turn in. Now, as you start to use the right lever, pull your inside knee in and brace your knees and legs into the tank and fairing. You can now brake extremely hard with your arms reasonably relaxed. This will help to make the bike more stable under braking as your body weight is being transferred into the bike rather than over the top of it. A further benefit from using your legs to brace against braking is that forearm pump will never occur, so you can enter the corner more smoothly and with better control.

On really fast straights that lead into tight hairpins, the urge to brake harder and later becomes even stronger.

"Use of the legs is something that people don't seem to see," says Nicky Hayden. "Most normal street bike riders watching in the crowd or at home on TV would think that we don't use our legs at all, that we're just sitting there. But the legs are what I use the most when braking."

Its faster to brake a little earlier. Begin braking a little sooner and more progressively, so you start gently, build up the braking forces and then tail them off when your

Dani Pedrosa getting his body weight down and forward to the inside of the bike to allow him to hold a tighter line and get the bike leaned over as little as possible – even though his knee will be dragging on the floor! Subtle? Absolutely.

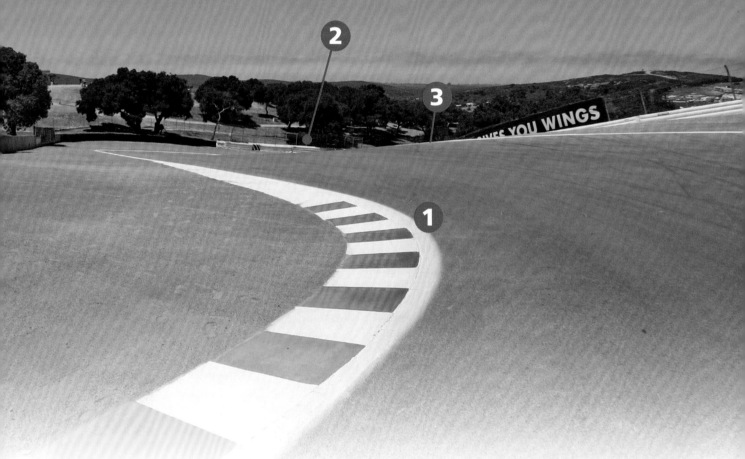

> "I'VE ALWAYS HAD THIS THING THAT IF I CAN CONNECT THE DOTS THEN I'M DOING GOOD LAPS. I GUESS THOSE DOTS ARE EACH BRAKING POINT, APEX AND EXIT POINT."
> COLIN EDWARDS

**The infamous Corkscrew at Laguna Seca. The combination of a blind turn-in and a steep drop with another turn at the bottom makes this a challenging corner, even for the professionals. Having marker points on the entry, on the crest and beyond help the rider to be confident going over the drop and down to the right-hander afterwards. You need to be positive with the throttle and this will only come from knowing where you are and where you want to go, even if you cannot see it yet! In 2005 Colin Edwards succeeded in joining all the dots here on his way to beating team-mate Valentino Rossi.**

speed is set. If we were to show on a graph the pressure used, it would look like a smooth rise and fall rather than a sudden, steep spike. This progression allows the bike's suspension to cope better with the forces generated and keep the bike stable as you transfer from braking forces to cornering forces.

Another important factor is where you're going to brake. Without exception the one point of reference for all top racers is a braking marker. A braking marker is the place where the braking starts, where the lever is applied and the start of the setting of speed for the corner takes place.

Each rider knows the exact, precise spot where they're going to get on the brakes for each corner, at every track across the world. Seeing this point from the distance is the key to them setting up for the corner. This is the point from which all their

actions are taken and made. Without one they would be lost. Without one they'd struggle with the corner. Without one they couldn't go fast.

"I've always had this thing that if I can connect the dots then I'm doing good laps," says Colin Edwards. "I guess those dots really are each braking point, apex and exit point."

There are many hundreds of different things that can be used for a braking marker, but they need to be fixed points – as with all timing references. In the case of braking, they need to be close to the track or actually on it. The further away from the track they are, then the less accurate they become. A tyre mark on the track surface would be a good braking marker, as would an identifiable feature in the grass to the side of the track. A 100-metre board is all right as a marker, but these boards tend to be further away from the track, so the accuracy reduces. A shadow, while easy to see, will obviously cause problems as the day wears on, the clouds arrive or it rains. There's a great urban legend of a racer who one day used a stone as his braking marker only to find that his braking got more and more wild as the laps passed. On closer inspection at the end of the race he discovered that his stone was in fact a tortoise moving towards the corner!

Remember that setting your speed for the corner is the ultimate objective. The faster you can go in, the faster your mid-corner speed will be and the faster you can come out at the exit. Of course this is relative to the 'in fast out slow; in slow out fast' rule described earlier.

Let's close this section with a word of advice from Chaz Davis: "Sometimes I find my line at a certain circuit by trial and error, and experience. But I mainly work it out by following other riders who are faster and watching what they do."

## STEERING

One thing has become very clear to me in talking to MotoGP riders about steering: they have developed the process of steering a bike from a conscious action into a subconscious one.

Here's Nicky Hayden on the subject of counter-steering: "It's not something for me that you can draw on a chalkboard. As far as counter-steering

and body-steering go, I think a lot of riders guess and don't really know what they do or don't understand. I mean, I just try to get around the track as fast as I can!"

It proves the point that when you first learn to do something it requires an awful lot of thought and concentration to get the job done. But the more you do it, the easier it becomes.

A good example is to think back to the first time you rode a motorcycle. You probably had someone there to help you with the basic control actions of starting the bike, using the throttle and the clutch in combination to get the bike moving. Looking from throttle to clutch and back again is common to see in novice riders as they work out the timing of letting the clutch out. Chances are that you looked too. Remember?

But now you give hardly any thought to this procedure. It has become instinctive. As John Hopkins says about counter-steering: "Erm, erm, it's just, erm, I dunno! It's just natural."

And here comes the twist. If it's instinctive, requiring no thought at all, then how do you make it better? Racing starts are a good example of the need to bring the control actions back into the conscious so you can make an improvement. You cannot change what you don't know – that's one of the certainties of life.

So what is steering? It's the process used to

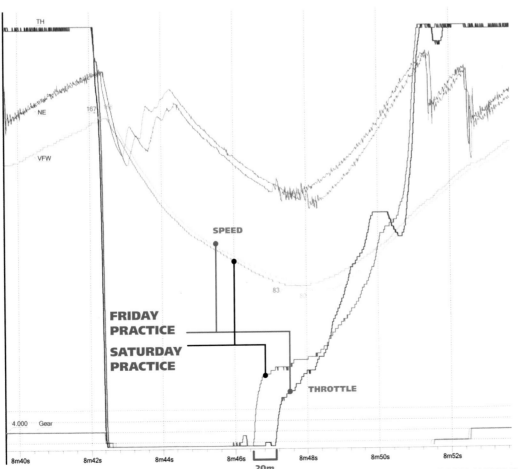

FRIDAY PRACTICE

SATURDAY PRACTICE

SPEED

THROTTLE

TH
NE
167
VFW
83
4.000  Gear
8m40s   8m42s   8m44s   8m46s   8m48s   8m50s   8m52s
20m

A readout from Thomas Lüthi's data-logging from the MotoGP at Le Mans in 2006. The readings were taken from two wet free practice sessions on the Friday and the Saturday and then overlaid. What we can see is absolute proof that if you go in fast you come out slow, and vice versa.

On the Friday trace you can see from the speed line that Thomas is able to carry speed into the turn but the application of the throttle is later in the corner, making the exit speed slower.

On the Saturday trace the speed into the corner is slower but the throttle can be applied earlier and therefore the speed out of the corner is higher. Also the slowest speed in the turn has increased from 80kph to 83kph. Remember that this data is from two very wet sessions – the difference in the dry would probably be even greater.

**Pushing your shoulder into the corner, as Kawasaki rider Shinya Nakano does, effectively puts pressure on the inside handlebar which, ultimately, makes the bike turn. The body movement alone wouldn't be sufficient to get the bike to turn.**

get the bike leant over so it can follow your chosen arc right through a corner.

I think we can all agree that if you want your bike to get round a corner at speed then lean angle is required.

The process by which you make the bike lean into the turn is called counter-steering – steering the bike counter to the direction of the corner. So, if you want to make the bike go left you have to turn the steering to the right. If you want the bike to go right then you have to turn the steering to the left.

Here are two expert quotes on the subject. Thomas Luthi: "When I'm turning right I push on the right bar. Sometimes if the corner is really fast then I pull on the left one too but not very often." Colin Edwards: "I think it depends on the speed – at 100mph I definitely counter-steer. I pull a little bit right to go left."

Now, I got my Physics O-Level at school and I've spoken to riders with a degree in the subject, but no-one I've discussed

this with is 100 per cent sure how and why this works. But to be honest it's more important to understand that it does work – and that it's the only way to get the bike to turn into a corner – than why it works.

To make counter-steering even easier to use as a tool, remember this: if you want to turn right you push on the right handlebar, and if you want to turn left you push on the left handlebar. You can, of course, pull on the outside bar instead, or push and pull at the same time: the effect – getting the front wheel to point away from the corner – is the same.

I prefer to push, for two reasons.

Firstly, pushing right to go right is easy for my humble grey matter to deal with. Secondly, we're normally slowing down into a corner,

so it's easier to use the deceleration forces to push on the bar rather than pull it.

Now, this isn't to say that pulling is wrong, or even that pushing and pulling at the same time is wrong – they're not. What's important is that you get the bike on to its line as quickly as possible, by making your steering action quick and positive.

The quicker you can turn the bike, the better: it gives you more options to play with at the beginning of the corner. The quicker you can turn the bike, the faster you can go into the corner. Think about the last time you went into a corner too fast. What was it too fast for? What action could you not perform at that speed? Getting the bike turned.

If you'd had the confidence to turn the bike quickly at that speed, would you

## "I USE MY BODY. I PUSH MY SHOULDER TO THE INSIDE OF THE CORNER."
SHINYA NAKANO

# The Good
## WHEN IT ALL GOES RIGHT

Smooth, and – to put it another and more important way – stable. Once the bike's stable, the rider feels much more confident in all areas. Even if the bike's sliding, it's still stable. Here, Makoto Tamada has managed to get his Honda into the apex of the corner with the bike in a stable condition. We can see this because he has the bike right where he wants it, with his knee over the kerbing. He's also carrying a lot of lean angle, which may not be the best thing as it might restrict his ability to drive the bike out of the corner due to the grip he's using to maintain that amount of lean.

# The Bad
## WHEN IT ALL GOES WRONG

Even the very best can get it wrong – a rare moment from World Champion Valentino Rossi. With his outside leg completely off the bike, there's now no way he can stay on it. This is a crash in the making. Luckily for Rossi, it'll be a lowside, so he's unlikely to get injured. From the position of the bike in relationship to the corner, we can also see that he has lost grip from the front and the rear of the bike at the same time, most likely due to the lean angle he has tried to use. Excessive lean angle is the one thing that will make a tyre lose its battle with the cornering forces acting upon it.

# The Ugly
## FAST, BUT...

Jumping around all over the bike and making big changes in your body's movement will make the bike more unstable. Troy Bayliss was one of the more animated riders on a MotoGP bike, using his body a lot to try and control the bike as it moved around beneath him. There's a twist to this: the more you move about and get aggressive with the bike, the more unstable it becomes, and the more you try to fight it. Yes, body movement is required to get the best from the bike, but knowing how much and when to do it is the key. Smooth and controlled movement on the bike makes the job easier.

have made the corner? Would your bike have coped? Of course.

You could also have the option, if you could get the bike turned more quickly, to move your turn entry point to later into the corner. This has the added benefit of making your line straighter through the corner. A straighter line allows you to keep the bike more upright, therefore giving you more grip. It allows the suspension to work better as the reduced lean angle means more suspension travel. The more you lean a bike over on its side, the more the suspension has to compress to cope with the cornering forces trying to push the bike towards the outside. This also doubles up to give you even more grip: the suspension can work better, allowing the load on the tyres to be reduced, therefore making a loss of traction less likely. With the bike a little more upright, you can apply the throttle a little earlier, thus giving you more drive on the exit of the corner and a few vital extra miles per hour in the middle of the corner.

All this comes from your ability to use the handlebars and counter-steer the bike quickly.

Putting pressure on the inside footpeg to try to get the bike to turn is a waste of time and effort. Logic should dictate that putting more of your body mass on the inside peg will get the bike to lean, and experimentation in a car park

or in really slow turns would support this theory. But once your bike gets up to speed and the strong gyroscopic forces from the front and rear wheels come into play, then the only thing that putting pressure on the inside peg will do is make your thighs a bit bigger!

Just leaning into the corner and hoping that the bike will follow is also a waste of time and effort. I'll admit that doing this can give you a slight change of direction, but will it make the bike turn? Will this alone get the bike into and out of a corner? The answer is 'no'. You'd need to have the turning arc of an oil tanker for this to work – and that isn't going to be of much use, or very exciting, for a bike.

But even MotoGP riders aren't too sure – or even in agreement with each other – on some of the essential steering points. Here, to conclude, are the views of three current stars.

Chris Vermeulen: "Your bike's handlebars, of course, play the big part in steering, but your footpegs help you to steer the bike too."

Loris Capirossi: "I have small levers; my arms are shorter so I haven't as much power as Gibernau, so I use my body and legs as well. I move and use a lot of leg like if you were to break a stone."

Shinya Nakano: "I use my body: I push my shoulder to the inside of the corner."

Loris Capirossi with his knee skimming the ground. The knee slider allows the rider to judge his lean angle. It's another valuable tool that the rider uses, and another thing that he thinks about as he goes through the corner. If he feels too much pressure on the knee, then he'll know the bike is sliding at both front and rear, and he'll need to make subtle adjustments before he ends up on the floor.

# SLIDING

**Government health warning:
smokers smile wider and ride faster**

The harder you get on the throttle towards the end of the turn, the more likely you are to get the rear of the bike to slide. MotoGP riders use this to change line in the corner as and when they want. The nice thing about a motorcycle is when it's sliding at the rear the front end is already set to turn into the slide – if the rider lets it. It's all part of the skill of steering with the rear – and as we all know a rear-end slide is easier to control than a front-end slide.

Sliding the rear of a motorcycle is one of the best feelings in the world – and world-class riders have the experience and confidence to do it at will. But it's not always the fastest way, even if it does look fabulous on TV. Like most riding skills it becomes a tool in the hands of a master craftsman.

With the big four-strokes in MotoGP and powerful four-strokes in World Superbikes and World SuperSport 600s, the art of rear-wheel steering is becoming more and more important, to the point where traction control, while making things safer for the rider, doesn't necessarily make the bike faster.

"Traction control limits the throttle opening," says James Ellison, "so even if you have the throttle fully open, on 100 per cent, the bike will only give you 80 per cent. So if you want to slide it, you have to move the position of the traction control so you get more power. You have to work with the bike: you can't just get on it and go as fast as you want because there are a lot of things on the bike that won't actually let you do that. You have to adapt your riding skills to suit how the bike has been developed. For me this is the biggest change I found when I started riding a real MotoGP bike."

A rider who can play around with the rear of his bike as it slides out of a corner has mastered the art of rear-wheel steering. But because of the risk of a highside and because of our natural reaction with the throttle in this situation, it's something that we need to get comfortable with. Riding off-road and riding SuperMoto bikes helps you to get used to the feel of a bike sliding in low-traction conditions.

At the California Superbike Schools, we have a bike called the Slide Machine. This bike has a pair of hydraulic outriggers fitted to it so that a rider can experience a rear-wheel slide with a greatly reduced chance of highsiding. Normally the first time a rider slides the rear of his bike he'll slam the throttle closed. This allows the tyre to grip the surface very suddenly – which in turn compresses the suspension. When the suspension unloads it literally catapults the rider over the highest side of the bike. A highside isn't one of the best crashes you can have.

But sliding the rear wheel does have several advantages. It's the ultimate in throttle control. It tightens the end of a corner, or indeed any part of a corner if you're really good at it. It allows you to still ride fast with reduced grip. And, of course, it looks so cool!

At some point or other almost every rider has lost traction at the rear tyre and the back of his bike has stepped out. This is a definite 'moment' when it occurs and can only be induced by incorrect throttle application in relationship to the amount of traction available.

Makoto Tamada is playing with the throttle here as his Honda gets sideways in the rain. Look at the throttle hand: even if he pinned it at this stage the bike would be unlikely to crash as it's upright. However, it wouldn't get much drive in these conditions, hence his throttle hand trying to apply as much as possible.

**1** As the rear of the bike starts to slide, our natural reaction is to reduce speed because it all starts happening too quickly. Obviously, to our stretched minds, we must close the throttle as this was the root cause of the problem we now face.

**2** As the slide gets worse, the forces start to act on the body and we close the throttle – and now the bike gets more out of shape. Here the rider's foot is already off the outside footpeg, making the chances of recovery slim.

**3** With the throttle closed, the suspension loads up as the tyre grips and then, like a giant catapult, it unloads all of its stored energy and flings the rider over the higher side of the bike, thus highsiding him.

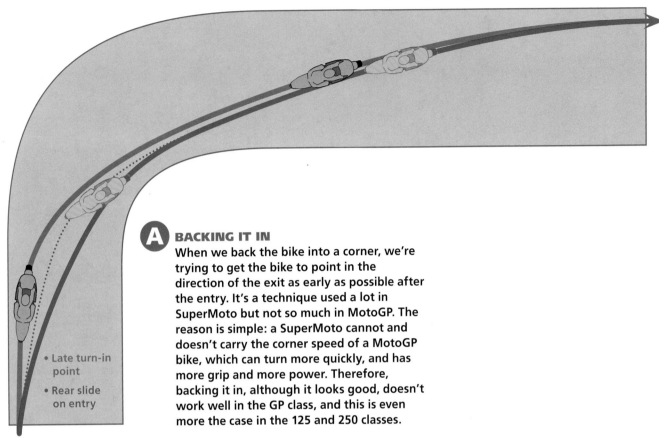

- Late turn-in point
- Rear slide on entry

### A BACKING IT IN

When we back the bike into a corner, we're trying to get the bike to point in the direction of the exit as early as possible after the entry. It's a technique used a lot in SuperMoto but not so much in MotoGP. The reason is simple: a SuperMoto cannot and doesn't carry the corner speed of a MotoGP bike, which can turn more quickly, and has more grip and more power. Therefore, backing it in, although it looks good, doesn't work well in the GP class, and this is even more the case in the 125 and 250 classes.

The situation the rider creates in this way can get even worse if he continues to use the throttle poorly. Once the back of the bike steps away, the right response is to check the throttle but not close it. Slamming the right hand shut as fast as possible just makes the rear tyre gain traction far too quickly – which could result in a crash as the suspension loads and then unloads, making the tyre break away again. If the back of the bike should step out, checking the throttle by keeping the throttle hand still will allow the rear tyre to regain traction much more progressively.

The other alternative – and the one used by these MotoGP riding gods – is to get on the throttle harder! This keeps the tyre spinning, thus tightening the corner so that the rider can, in effect, make the track a lot wider on the way out and therefore carry even more exit speed. And we wonder why these guys are paid so much money!

But it also carries the greatest risk to man and machine – the highside.

James Ellison is mystified as to why so many riders do highside: "When people highside I think, 'How did you do that?' You should know when it's going to go, so use a little bit of rear brake or roll off a little – you shouldn't shut off! I've only ever had two highsides."

Steering with the rear wheel is all about good throttle control. The more throttle you try to apply while the bike is leant over, the greater the chance of the back tyre losing grip and spinning. Watch world-class riders and you'll notice that all of them, without exception, get the bike sliding in the final part of the turn when the bike is starting to come more and more upright. If you tried to slide a bike at the apex of a corner, the point at which your lean angle is greatest, you'd spin the rear very suddenly and fall off. Aggressive throttle roll-on must be left until the exit of the turn.

This is where riders use their body weight to allow them to slide the bike and still get drive and hold the line on the exit of the turn. Loris Capirossi: "It's very important to pick the bike up as early as you can. And this is why I keep my body inside and pick up the bike, so from the middle of the corner my body stays out. Then the bike is straight and you open the throttle – perfect!"

Many riders confuse the feeling of the rear suspension compressing as a slide. The sensation is similar, but when the tyre is spinning the suspension actually unloads and works more efficiently over bumps. When the tyre is close to breaking away, the suspension is taking a large load from the throttle application. This is the point just before the tyre starts to slide.

There are also two different levels of sliding: full-on 'slideways' showboating and much more

- Running wide on exit

- Rear slide on exit

**B** **SPINNING UP ON EXIT**
One area where MotoGP riders excel is getting the bike turned in more tightly by sliding the rear wheel. As can be seen in the diagram, if a MotoGP rider runs wide he gets on the throttle even harder to make the rear tyre lose traction and bring the back end of the bike round (to the outside of the corner), thus straightening the last part of the line and preventing him running wide. And sometimes we wonder why they're paid so well...

"IT'S VERY IMPORTANT TO PICK THE BIKE UP AS EARLY AS YOU CAN. AND THIS IS WHY I KEEP MY BODY INSIDE AND PICK UP THE BIKE, SO FROM THE MIDDLE OF THE CORNER MY BODY STAYS OUT. THEN THE BIKE IS STRAIGHT AND YOU OPEN THE THROTTLE – PERFECT!"
LORIS CAPIROSSI

Marco Melandri getting out of a turn with smoke pouring off the rear tyre. He's already tucked up behind the screen and has the throttle open to the stop to get off down the straight. It looks awesome – but there's going to be little drive and too much slide.

subtle drive lines, where a faint line of rubber appears from the rear tyre as the rider comes out of the corner.

Once the rear wheel steps out of line from the front, you're in a full-on MotoGP-style slide. You may not be smoking the rear, but you'll nevertheless be sliding. You'll feel the back of the bike out of line with the front because your bum will be moving to the outside of the corner while your handlebars are turning to match and correct the slide. That's right, if you leave the bike to its own devices it'll steer into the slide and self-correct. If you grab hold of the bars the bike can't do this and the slide will increase. In a car we're taught that if the back end steps out we must turn the steering wheel into the slide

to regain control. The same ideal applies to a bike but it'll do it itself.

With the rear wheel spinning and sliding, you can play around with the slide by rolling on more or less throttle. But part of the art of sliding a bike is to know when you have to pick the bike up and into the slide so that you can still manage to get some drive while sliding. Again, look at the MotoGP racers and you'll see that they have their bodies down the inside of the bike while the bike is upright. This again allows them to get more drive and maintain the line they've chosen for the bike to run.

The mere mortal's choice for dealing with a rear-wheel slide – whether on a track or on the road – is to check the throttle. Don't roll it on or off – just keep it constant. By doing this, you make the throttle into a rev limiter and this allows the rear tyre to regain grip more gradually, thus preventing a highside.

## PUSHING THE FRONT

In terms of getting it right or wrong, pushing the front is the most risky of all the sliding techniques and it can end in a lowside very rapidly.

Pushing the front involves the front tyre carrying most of the weight of the bike into the first half of the turn, and in some cases right up to the apex. Given that the front tyre has the smaller contact patch, pushing the front is much harder to get right than sliding the rear, and the fine line between making it work and crashing is so thin that it beggars belief.

"The MotoGP style," says Colin Edwards, "is more to push both the front and rear at the same time, instead of just going in on the front. You're trying to load the front and rear almost simultaneously so at that point you're really working with both contact patches to get the bike to slow down."

To cite the example of Simon Crafar again, he was very good pushing the front and used it to brilliant effect in 1998 to set the lap record for a 500cc GP bike at Donington Park. He would go into the Old Hairpin, as he put it, "way too fast", and use the loaded weight on the front tyre to make it scrub across the track and therefore increase friction between the tyre and the surface, thus slowing down the bike in the early and middle part of the corner. It's a very high-risk strategy. The heavier the bike you're riding, the finer the line between slide and crash. On lighter bikes it's less difficult as the inertia of the bike's weight has less effect.

If you push it too far and feel that the front of the bike is going to fold on you and send you off into the gravel, then you really have only one plan of action – get back on the throttle. This will reduce the weight over the front and should help the bike to recover from what could be a terminal front-end loss.

This is a technique we see from time to time in MotoGP races. The best example I've ever seen was Jeremy McWilliams on the Proton at the Czech GP at Brno in 2002, as shown in the photo sequence on the right. Having his knee on the floor also helped him to balance the bike as the front tyre started to let go.

But it doesn't always work out. Kenny Roberts Jnr once tried this on his 500cc Suzuki in the last corner at Paul Ricard in France. He came into the turn and the front started to go, followed very quickly by the back. The bike was sliding at both ends across the track and KR Jnr was holding the weight of the bike on his knee. Unfortunately, when the tyres gripped they did so at the same time and slung him into one of the biggest highsides I've ever seen.

**1** It's gone! By rights at this point Jeremy McWilliams should be about to slide down the track in an ungraceful heap...

**2** ...but even with the front end about to tuck and his knee and elbow on the floor, the plucky Irishman hasn't given up yet.

**3** Holding the Proton's weight on his knee has allowed him the chance to try and recover. Having the outside leg locked into the bike is helping the situation as he also has a strong and stable point on the outside of the bike.

**4** Opening the throttle transfers weight off the front of the bike and towards the rear, allowing the front tyre to regain grip.

**5** Saved! And just in the nick of time. If you look at the distance travelled in these six shots, you'll get an insight into just how quickly these guys can think and react.

**6** No doubt with a much higher heart rate than before, McWilliams saves the Proton and himself from a visit to the gravel trap and a long walk back to the pits.

# RACING LINES

## Anyone who thinks there's only one racing line through a corner isn't a racer

**Coming into the first chicane at Le Mans, Shinya Nakano takes a line that might help him to overtake Ducati-mounted Loris Capirossi before the Italian rider starts to flick to the right.**

**Valentino Rossi has clear track in front of him, so he has a wider choice of lines than the defensive and aggressive lines taken by the riders behind him. He can concentrate on going as fast as he can to build a gap between him and the others.**

Meanwhile Dani Pedrosa has settled for the same line as Marco Melandri and will wait for another opportunity to pass the Italian rider.

So let's get one thing straight right from the off. For a motorcycle, there's no such thing as one ideal fast line through a corner. This is easily proven out on track and in races, as you can see lots and lots of overtaking. You can see the various different lines there are for any given corner by looking at the slide marks left by all the riders over a race weekend. There isn't just one big black line through all of the turns.

Although there are many variations in the lines that we have available to us, they can be dropped into three distinct categories.

### 1 THE QUALIFYING LINE

This line allows the rider to run a late turning-in point so that he can square off the corner and make the most of his drive on the exit. However, in a race this will leave the 'door' wide open for someone to overtake him on the inside of the corner. While the rider who performs the overtaking manoeuvre might run wide on the exit, it'll be hard for the overtaken rider to get back in front. Once someone comes down the inside, they'll tend to block you so that you cannot get on the throttle early enough to repass on the exit.

### 2 THE RACING LINE

The racing line falls somewhere between the qualifying line and the overtaking line. It's a compromise between entry speed, throttle control and defending your position on track.

Each line and its use is part of a rider's plan for the race. He uses it to make sure he doesn't show all of his cards to the opposition, leaving him able to speed up or slow down depending on the situation at hand. Racing requires that the rider rides at about 95 per cent, not 100 per cent as in qualifying. Trying to keep your concentration level high but not overloaded makes sure that you ride at this not-quite-balls-out level until the last few laps of the race, or even the very last lap. It's a game of chess that develops over the whole race.

In the photo, see how Carlos Checa (7) keeps wide so he can try and catch Sete Gibernau (15) and Nicky Hayden (69) by using the qualifying line.

### 3 THE OVERTAKING LINE

This line runs early into the corner and is designed to allow the rider to dive up the inside on the approach to a bend to make an overtaking pass. Because the bike is more upright for longer, it allows the rider to brake later, with less risk of losing traction on the front end.

The shape of the line does mean it's an in-fast-out-slow plan, but this is OK as the overtaken rider cannot repass because in most corners you'll be in the way blocking him. Unless he wants to hit you in the behind, he'll have to back out of the throttle and match, not exceed, your drive on the exit.

**1** THE QUALIFYING LINE

**2** THE RACING LINE

**3** THE OVERTAKING/DEFENSIVE LINE

To take advantage of each of these three basic lines, you'd better know where each of them will put you in the corner. To do this you need to have some points in the corners to make up your line. A line will consist of three basic parts: entry, apex and exit.

This will mean you have to be looking into a corner as you approach. But if you don't know what you should be looking at, then the whole process is a complete waste of time and effort – you'll be guessing your way around the corner.

"A lot of the time I use the big-picture method to get around a corner," says Chris Vermeulen. The big picture in this context is having a complete view of the corner in your head, like a cinema screen image, and matching that with what you see.

Looking into a turn might help you to try and decide what sort of corner it is: whether it's tightening up, opening up or staying constant, whether the surface is good, whether the surface is smooth or bumpy – but you can still be wasting all this information if you don't use some of it to decide *where you want to be...*

"When you ride a big, fast bike," says Valentino Rossi, "everything happens very fast, so you need to stay 100 per cent concentrated on what is going to happen next. You need to ride with your mind a little bit in front of the bike.

On the track I'm always thinking about the next corner."

Having an entry, apex and exit for any turn simply isn't good enough if you want to be a smooth and confident rider. Selecting something specific to mark all of these points will give you the edge you're looking for in the smoothness stakes.

John Hopkins makes a good point when he says: "The bikes get faster each and every year, but if I can stick to the braking markers that I've always used, then I'll get faster because the bikes approach faster and that means I'll be faster. There are certain points on the track where I turn in, where I pick it up and where I get on the throttle. One thing I try to avoid using are marks on the track because you can show up one year and find the track has been completely resurfaced! I would describe myself as a point A to point B rider. I like points but if you're on a qualifying lap, on the qualifying tyre, then you're definitely big picture... you're like, 'Well I just wanna be somewhere in the middle of the corner and somewhere where I can pin it wide open'.

"On the race tyre then I'm definitely point A to point B. I want to turn it in at the same place every lap; I wanna pick it up right there every lap. Of course, you're going to have some laps that differ because you'll be around somebody –

**The final turn at Sepang, Malaysia.** A hairpin like this can really show the differences in the types of line used by the riders. Differences are less obvious in a fast sweeper, where line variation is more subtle but still exists.

Chris Vermeulen keeping the bike nice and tight to the inside of the corner. He's judging his line by how close his knee is to the white paint on the inside. He made the decision to do that much earlier in the corner and is now looking towards the next turn.

someone will be ahead of you, and you might have to block them a little bit."

When you look at a corner, make a definite decision as to where you're going to turn the bike. – next to that tyre mark, kerb or third white line. Make a definite apex point so you'll know exactly where you want the bike to be in the middle of the corner, and, just as important, make a definite exit point too so you can really get comfortable with your throttle application and drive hard out of the corner.

Have you ever noticed how close to the edge of the kerb MotoGP riders get? They can do this because they're confident that they can put the bike in exactly the same spot on the exit time and time again.

You'll have to recognise these places as you make your way through the turn, but without them you'll find that the line you wanted, or tried to achieve, will be wide of the mark. This is something that we all do already to a greater or lesser degree, but developing the skill of putting the bike *exactly* where we want it to go is a sign of a rider who understands and can apply the art of line selection.

Not making a definite decision when to turn your bike into a corner will make the rest of the corner harder to get right.

Have you ever found yourself having to make

steering corrections in the middle and last part of a corner? Have you ever found yourself having to roll off or check the throttle in a corner? It happens a lot and one of the most common causes is a lack of turn-entry point.

Not knowing exactly where you want to turn your bike in, to begin the corner, leaves you open to falling foul of your instinctive reactions. Getting into a corner too early is one of these reactions. Firstly, none of us wants to run on – if we do go straight ahead then we really do know that we've got the corner very, very wrong indeed. This run-off danger area affects our decision to turn: the sooner we turn, the sooner we get away from it, so by the time we apex we're as far away from it as possible, making us feel safer on the entry of the corner.

The second thing that makes us turn early is looking into the corner! Now how screwed up is that? If you agree with the statement 'you go where you look', then the mere fact you're looking into the corner will mean that, to a greater or lesser degree, you'll start to turn into the corner. The result is a very comfortable first part of the corner but a middle part and exit that requires plenty of steering correction and throttle correction – neither of which is going to enhance your ability to get on the throttle hard at the end of the corner.

"WHEN YOU RIDE A BIG, FAST BIKE, EVERYTHING HAPPENS VERY FAST, SO YOU NEED TO STAY 100 PER CENT CONCENTRATED ON WHAT IS GOING TO HAPPEN NEXT. YOU NEED TO RIDE WITH YOUR MIND A LITTLE BIT IN FRONT OF THE BIKE. ON THE TRACK I'M ALWAYS THINKING ABOUT THE NEXT CORNER."
**VALENTINO ROSSI**

THE VANISHING POINT GIVES THE ILLUSION THAT THE SURFACE YOU'RE RIDING ON DISAPPEARS. IT CAN BE CREATED BY A CREST, AN OBSTRUCTION OR WHERE THE INSIDE AND OUTSIDE KERBS APPEAR TO MEET. THIS IS USEFUL INFORMATION AS THE VANISHING POINT MOVES THROUGH THE CORNER WITH THE RIDER'S EYES. THIS WILL ALLOW THE RIDER TO GATHER MAXIMUM INFORMATION ABOUT THE TURN MOST EFFICIENTLY, THUS GIVING HIM MORE SPACE AND THEREFORE MORE TIME.

The key to both problems is to decide when you want to start the corner by picking a marker of some description to use each and every lap.

But there's another twist to the selection of lines. You must have the ability to change your line as and when circumstances dictate. For example, a bike goes down and leaves oil on the track. The circuit and marshals clear it all up but there's still a cement dust line where the worst of the oil was dropped. This, of course, is on your ideal line for the corner. So now you have to find a new way around that corner – it may be a compromise or you may even find that your new line is even better than the one you had before!

Valentino Rossi is an excellent example of a rider who can adapt and change his line as and when required. Whatever line he picks, he has the ability to change it at will. This can be done by changing the turn-in point, the apex or the exit – or sometimes all three! It'll definitely mean that he'll have to change his braking points, how far into the corner he brakes, and when and how he gets on the throttle – but he can and does do this, even in a race. The key to this ability is to know the track intimately.

Most racers have a line that they know and they stick to it regardless of whether it works, needs changing or rethinking completely. However, the more experimentation we do with our lines, the better our knowledge of the track and the more options we have to make changes as and when required.

Part of the ability to be able to do this depends on how well we can discipline our eyes.

The faster we go, the faster it feels – until we get to a point where we think we're going really, really fast when in fact we discover that we've slowed down. A strange thing happens to motorcyclists when we decide to go fast – we restrict the amount of space we have to work in.

The moment we start to increase the pace, our vision moves down and closer to the front of the bike, giving us the impression that we're going faster than we actually are. Think how your perception of speed changes when you have less physical space: 60mph feels much faster on a narrow tree-lined country lane than on a wide open motorway; or if you ride into a tunnel you suddenly feel you're travelling much more quickly. The physical space is reduced – and the same effect can come about from the way we naturally use our eyes.

It's very easy to find yourself up against this barrier and it's a perfectly understandable instinct as we humans are really only designed to travel at about 11mph, not 70mph plus leant over with our knees skimming the deck and coping with the centrifugal forces generated by cornering. It's no

wonder we revert back to what our body thinks is comfortable.

But this reaction is the most limiting factor to our ability to ride a motorcycle through a corner at speed, and something on which I worked very hard with Thomas Lüthi to get him to his 125 world title in 2005. Thomas's vision was always hooked up on the apex and getting him to move his vision to a place on the exit once the bike was set on its line was one of the major breakthroughs in his riding. He was able to get on the throttle earlier and more progressively as a result.

When you see a MotoGP rider in a slow corner, where's he looking? Is it down to the apex or is it as far ahead as possible? It'll be the latter, in order to generate more space for himself so that he can follow the throttle plan he believes to be the best for a faster lap time.

You should raise your head and look as far up and into the corner as you can so that you have the maximum amount of room to use rather than restricting it by looking too close to the bike. Try riding along in a straight line and look a few metres in front of the mudguard – see how fast you can go before you feel uncomfortable. Now look down the track as far as you can see and you'll go twice as fast with half the stress.

The place where you should be looking is called the vanishing point. It's the place where the inside

**Nicky Hayden looking to his next turn. It's not only important to recognise what you look at but what it means to you. If it has no meaning then it becomes a distraction. A distraction can cost you vital tenths of a second in a corner. Your eyes should always be ahead of the bike. Look to where you want to go, not where you're going.**

and outside kerbs or sides of the road or track appear to meet and make the tarmac 'vanish', so that all you can see beyond is grass or gravel – certainly no surface to ride on. Looking for the vanishing point maximises the amount of room you can have in any given corner. Make sure you're always looking for it, because the unique thing the vanishing point does – unlike all of your other points – is move through the corner as you ride through. It's a bit like chasing a rainbow. You'll never get to the pot of gold, but what you will get is command of the space in front of you and therefore a much better lap time.

The combination of having good marker points and applying good control of your eyes will produce much better results than any throttle application, any sliding or any braking you do.

At the California Superbike School we spend the whole of one level working on the eyes as it's such an important area. With your eyes working correctly out on track, you'll feel a lot more confident with what you can do. However, like breathing, it's something that we don't even think about. We need training and we need to be ready and willing to change to make sure we can get the benefits. There are several visual drills you can try out in the *Twist of the Wrist* series of books by American riding guru Keith Code. I highly recommend that you get these books and read

through and practise these drills as they do make such a huge difference. But, as we've said before, it really does take a lot of hard work.

When training professional riders, the biggest barrier to these guys going faster can be throttle control, braking, how quickly they can turn the bike, their lines through a corner, drive on the exit, and so on. On the face of it, any one of these problems can be tackled as an individual point, but when you look more deeply into the issue you'll discover that 99 times out of 100 the reason there's a barrier there results from a visual problem, not a physical one.

The eyes can also lead you to believe that there aren't any camber changes on the track. Once you're leant over in a turn, it's harder to see exactly how much camber you have to play with. Imagine you're leant over in a corner at 20 degrees and the corner has a camber of five degrees. Do you think it would look cambered or flat to the naked, leant-over eye? It would be the same if the corner has neutral camber (ie, it's flat); would it look like flat to you if you even had 10 degrees of lean angle?

This gives you good reason to walk the track to see exactly where the cambers are. It'll save you time and money in the long run as you'll have a much better throttle plan as a result. Of course, you could do it by feel as well, but that takes

**Even on his scooter Valentino Rossi is looking into the turn. Even at these slow speeds he can gather useful information about the corner. It may or may not work when he rides through at MotoGP speeds, but it does give him a solid starting point. He should, of course, be wearing a helmet...**

The Corkscrew at Laguna Seca is a challenging turn for the eyes. Max Biaggi (3) is looking at Troy Bayliss (12) and Sete Gibernau (15), and is likely to be thinking that his chosen overtaking line wasn't such a good call. We can tell this because he's looking at the riders he might collide with rather than the line he wanted to use.

**1** On the approach to the Corkscrew at Laguna Seca the track has a tiny amount of positive camber, allowing the bike to push against it.

**2** However, when riding through the top of the Corkscrew the camber goes flat for a very short period. It just happens to be the part of the corner where the rider is starting to change direction for the right-hander.

**3** As the rider changes direction and begins to drop down the steep Corkscrew, the camber starts to go positive again...

**4** ...and when the rider gets leant over to the right, the camber and drop help the bike to dig into the surface better. However, if you're off the throttle the camber and drop will overwork the front tyre and cause loss of traction, as happened to Mick Doohan here. You need to start opening the throttle as soon as the bike is turned.

longer and can be a lesson learned the hard way!

Cambers on the track can be our friend or enemy. The trouble is that unless we come across a really extreme camber change, we don't really take much notice or take advantage of this crucial piece of track design.

In every corner you ride you'll encounter three types of camber: positive, negative and neutral.

### POSITIVE CAMBER

This is when the outside edge of the corner is higher than the inside. This is the best kind of camber for a bike because the forces that try to push you to the outside are countered more strongly by the banking of the turn. It means you can run into the corner faster as you ride into the camber, like a wall of death. Be aware, though, that all corners with positive camber will flatten out on the exit, requiring measured throttle application as the camber reduces to neutral or even negative, depending on what sort of day the track designer had when he got to that turn...

### NEUTRAL CAMBER

This is when the surface is completely flat – and actually it's quite rare because this type of surface doesn't drain very well. As a result track designers are reluctant to use neutral camber, although it can add an extra challenge to a corner.

### NEGATIVE CAMBER

This is the worst kind of camber because the bike has nothing to push against when it's leant over because the outside of the turn is lower than the inside. It means that we use more lean angle for a given speed and this in turn reduces how much throttle we can use. Conversely this type of corner looks more daunting than it is because our lean angle makes it appear worse.

### COMBINED CAMBERS

Some devious track designers put a combination of cambers all in one turn. This creates a real challenge. Knowing when to use the throttle harder and when to be cautious becomes an art.

If you want to learn more about cambers, the *MCN Circuit Guide* is a good source of information for UK race tracks and will save you the long walk before your next track day or race.

Nevertheless, motorcycles and riders do sometimes clash in what's required from each of them to make the best job of the corner, and body positioning is a prime example.

Getting your knee on the floor to judge and gauge your lean angle (the true reason for knee sliding) has more to do with how you hang off than it does with how far the bike is leant over. OK, so you'll never achieve plastic sliding heaven with your bike totally upright, but I've lost count

Negative camber (where the inside of the corner is higher than the outside) creates greater demand on the tyre and the amount of grip it can offer the rider. The corner drops away and the tyre doesn't have a 'wall' to push against to help it with the cornering forces generated and is therefore more likely to slide. Careful throttle control is required in these types of turns.

**1** In an ideal world the spine should be in line with or slightly to the inside of the bike. If it's the other way, then the rider creates too much pressure on the inside handlebar – which will cause the bike to move off line.

**2** The knee and the thigh should be able to help the rider lock into the bike better, allowing him to hold his body weight with the leg, not rest his weight on the handlebar. Here the shape of the fuel tank is hindering the rider's ability to lock in effectively. If the rider moved back from the fuel tank a little it would help.

**3** The inside foot should be tucked up and out of the way, but the outside foot should be used to help to push the knee and thigh into the fuel tank. This can mean using the ball of the foot or even the arch, depending on the length of the rider's shin and the position of the cut-out in the fuel tank.

of the number of times I've heard these words: "I can get my pegs, toes and even exhaust can on the floor, but I never touch my knee down."

If this is you then let's clear up one thing. *You have enough lean.* Grinding anything else into the tarmac will just result in a crash. There's always a fine balancing act that goes on between corner speed and lean angle. The more speed you carry in the corner, the further you have to lean the bike over. Taking a corner at 10mph won't require you to drag your knee or anything else on the floor; you could do it but it would be a complete waste of time. Taking a tight corner at 100mph, however, will require a lot of lean!

The biggest problem most riders face is when they try and 'push' their knee towards the ground they normally end up rotating their hip around the back of the fuel tank and this pushes their leg up along the fairing instead of towards the ground where it needs to be. On a MotoGP bike there's so much grip that you'll see riders with their knees wedged between the fairing and the ground!

Your leg should be relaxed so that it drops towards the floor, and to achieve this you need to have a good anchor position on the outside of the bike with your other leg. A good anchor has other benefits. You can reduce the input on the handlebars and keep your upper body more relaxed too. This helps the bike to handle better.

In fact, you don't have a good anchor unless you can let go of the handlebars but still remain on the bike.

Try this. Put you bike on a paddock stand. You can use the side stand but in this case get someone to hold the bike for you so that if you get it wrong the bike doesn't fall over. Some Italian motorcycle stands struggle to hold the weight of the bike let alone that of the rider too.

Now hang off in your normal style. Got there? Good. Now let go of the handlebars.

If you come crashing to the ground in an undignified heap, you didn't have a good anchor point with your outside leg. You should use those indents in the fuel tank to hold on with – that's what they're there for. Fitting Stomp pads helps as well. A Stomp pad is a clear pad that has lots of little knobbles on the surface. These knobbles get into the nooks and crannies of your leathers and help your grip the tank. Thomas Lüthi, Leon Camier, Sandro Cortese and Dani Pedrosa all use these pads on their bikes to help their lock-in and reduce rider fatigue.

"I've been doing it so long that locking-in isn't really an issue," states Colin Edwards. "But when you're doing 200mph and pulling your head out of the bubble it gets a little windy!"

If you can't lock into the tank very well, try shifting your heel up to force your knee into that

"I TRY TO KEEP MY
HELMET BEHIND THE
SCREEN. SOMETIMES I
PUT MY HEAD TO THE
INSIDE AND IT FEELS
NOT SO GOOD."
**SHINYA NAKANO**

In the first few laps of a race the line you want can be compromised by other riders being in your way or on your ideal line. One way to help combat this is to have a variety of lines that you can use in the first lap or two. This gives you more options and is better than the 'make it up as you go along' approach. Have a line plan.

indent in the tank. Some bikes are better than others in this respect. The Kawasaki ZX6R and Honda SP2 are good ones. Bikes that are harder than others are the Ducati 999 and 916. On the 999 it's more due to the design of the 'bucket' seat unit, which twists the hip and therefore moves the outside leg away from the tank, making it harder to lock in place securely.

Make sure that you don't slide your wedding tackle around the back of the fuel tank. It might feel all right but it twists your body and forces your inside leg into the fairing and outside leg into the air. Ruben Xaus and Colin Edwards are examples of riders who do this. Always aim for a gap the size of a fist between the back of the tank and your wedding tackle – something like 5 to 6 inches should be all that you need. By the way, adding a pad to the back of the tank doesn't solve the problem as you need that gap in order to move your hip at 90 degrees to the bike; a pad simply extends the back of the fuel tank and therefore doesn't resolve the issue.

Practise locking into the bike until it feels comfortable and then go out and try it on the

move. You might feel a lot of tension in the outside leg – that's OK. This shows that you're using the right muscles to hang on – so you can hang off!

Now all you have to do is add lean – the rest will follow naturally.

Lean angles look crazy on GP bikes, and they are! Getting a bike leant over that far at speed is the result of a fine balancing act from the rider. The more speed he has to carry through the corner, the more lean he needs to counter the cornering forces that are trying to push the bike to the outside of the turn. It's the front and rear tyres that keep the bike on the track so the grip they have is very important. The more grip, the more lean angle you can have – but the tyre can only do so much. Overstep the limits of the tyre and the bike will slide on the front or rear, or both.

So the rider has to achieve a fine balance between lean and speed. If he can get the bike to be more upright in the corner then he has some lean angle to play with. Therefore he can add more speed because he can lean the bike over more. However, as he adds more speed he

has to lean further over. And so the balancing act takes place. In qualifying you see this more often from more riders as they go for that one really fast lap.

Another body position aspect that can often be seen in novice racing is a rider pushing the bike away and underneath him, like a motocross rider. Inexperienced riders do this to try and trick themselves into thinking that they aren't actually leaning over too far.

The reality is that doing this makes the bike use significantly more lean angle than it needs, reducing the level of traction and the ability to use the throttle – which in turn makes the bike less stable. Add to this your body mass sitting on the wrong side of the bike's centre of mass and you can soon see how this is going to go wrong in less time than it takes to try and recover from the situation.

It's akin to a passenger on your bike sitting upright in the middle of a corner. If you've ever experienced that you'll know how unstable the bike becomes. Well, you as the rider and racer should be getting your body down and to the inside of the bike. Look at pictures of the top-level boys and how many of them have their heads held over the high side of the bike? Some will place their heads behind the screen, but most have their heads hanging down and to the inside of the bike. This allows your spine to remain straight and parallel to the bike. The advantage you gain by doing this is that the inside arm can be bent and therefore there's no unwanted or unnecessary pressure on the handlebar as the bike goes through the corner.

Shinya Nakano is a good example of someone who keeps his head behind the screen: "I try to keep my helmet close to the centre of the screen. Sometimes I put my head to the inside and it feels not so good."

The trick that many riders play on themselves comes from their upper body being further away from the ground. The further away from that rushing tarmac their head is, surely the safer they are? Nope. It just means that when it all goes wrong they're going to have further to fall.

Having your spine parallel with the bike, like a good pillion, is what you should be striving for to get the best from your machine.

# MUGELLO
## ITALIAN GRAND PRIX

Mugello is one of the finest tracks in Europe both for the rider and the spectator.

### SAN DONATO
A serious challenge. You approach at close to 200mph and need a corner speed of around 80mph. Losing 120mph is demanding enough, but the approach to the turn is blind and it drops down as well. A downhill entry means the bike is less settled and has less grip as the ground drops away.

### POGGIO SECCO
What goes down must also come up, and after San Donato you have a sharp rise to Poggio Secco. This also has a blind approach but it goes flat before you turn in, making life a little easier. Getting drive up the hill is important. Just as you turn left you'll need to get ready for the next right.

### MATERASSI
The fast right-hander following Poggio Secco, making this the second half of the first chicane at Mugello. Having a good visual clue to aim at on the exit helps with drive here down the short straight. Thankfully there are loads, including a conveniently placed marshals' point.

### CASANOVA
We get another blind approach as the track drops into the valley. Casanova is less daunting as the drop is more gradual than at San Donato. However, you'll also be looking to accelerate down most of the corner and into Savelli.

### SAVELLI
One of the simpler corners on the track: it's unlikely you'll have to brake much here, depending on drive from Casanova of course. You should be turning somewhere close to the cut through to the short circuit.

### ARRABBIATA 1
Most Italian tracks have corners that are a real challenge and these two are no exception to that rule. To make matters worse this is one of the areas where Mugello badly needs resurfacing thanks to all the Formula One cars that test here. Make sure you're loose on the handlebars on the exit of the corner, where the bumps are at their worst.

### ARRABBIATA 2
Mugello's most difficult corner and the one that also holds the key to a good lap time. The corner itself isn't too much of a problem as it's fast and consistent. The challenge arises from the fact that, like a lot of other corners here, it's blind on the approach and exit.

### SCARPERIA
Another blind corner but this time heading downhill again. Here you need a good line to make sure you're in the right place on the exit, not too far to the outside.

### PALAGIO
Another straightforward turn, with a slight downhill entry. Having a good exit marker to drive to is important to your lap time – the end of the gravel is a good starting point.

### CORRENTAIO
A long looping right-hander that's still dropping slightly and has the most gentle of all the elevation changes here. But it's hard on the eyes because it's so long. Getting a good apex helps you to carry more mid-corner speed.

### BIONDETTI
The quickest of all the chicanes and an absolute joy when you get it right. Flicking the bike from left to right at this speed is one hell of a thrill! Your speed here completely depends on your ability to turn the bike while accelerating.

### BUCINE
One of the longest, fastest left-handers in MotoGP. And guess what? It's also downhill. You need good drive on exit for strong speed down the long straight. Leading the corner with your eyes is also important and the inside wall helps you do this for most of the corner, certainly from the entry.

### STRAIGHT
Tuck in and give it all you've got!

© DORNA

80mph
(2nd gear)

SAN DONATO

190mph
(6th gear)

CORRENTAIO

70mph
(2nd gear)

BIONDETTI

80mph
(2nd gear)

PALAGIO

155mph
(4th gear)

SCARPERIA

70mph
(2nd gear)

125mph
(3rd gear)

95mph
(3rd gear)

ARRABBIATA 2

POGGIO SECCO

**70mph**
(2nd gear)

MATERASSI

**75mph**
(2nd gear)

**80mph**
(2nd gear)

BORGO SAN
LORENZO

**130mph**
(3rd gear)

**80mph**
(3rd gear)

CASANOVA

**160mph**
(5th gear)

SAVELLI

**85mph**
(3rd gear)

**125mph**
(3rd gear)

Award

ARRABBIATA 1

**100mph**
(3rd gear)

**60mph**
(2nd gear)

BUCINE

**120mph**
(3rd gear)

# QUALIFYING

An essential ingredient to winning and
where your feedback really counts

In qualifying you need to ride faster than you do in the race. This is all about getting the very, very best from yourself, your bike, your team and your tyres – for one blistering lap. With super-sticky qualifying tyres the whole way you ride the track will change. That extra grip gives you more options, but the twist is that you can only get one lap out of qualifying tyres before they're toasted. One lap to unlearn and relearn everything that went before...

**Qualifiers fitted and time to leave the garage and get ready for the fastest lap you can do. Qualifying is an important part of racing at national level and above. Getting just one extra place on the grid can help a rider achieve a higher finish. Some riders will sacrifice a qualifying session to help get better settings for the race, but if this means you're on the back of the grid...**

In much of racing, and certainly as you start to move up through the ranks, you'll need to get out there and start qualifying. Qualifying for me is the best part of racing both as a spectator, a riding coach and an ex-racer. It's when the riders and the teams really push to get the very best from all the component parts to achieve that one special lap. Faster than anything the rider will do in the race, faster than anyone has gone around that track at any time that weekend, and maybe even faster then ever before.

Texan Tornado Colin Edwards says: "Now we only have one qualifying session in MotoGP, it's much more important. But you have to make sure your race set-up is good first and foremost – that should be your number one priority. When you have more traction at the rear with a qualifying tyre that can sometimes create other problems – the extra grip changes everything. You go out on a qualifier and it's sometimes hard to get yourself to open it when you should. That's usually why the second qualifier is quicker than the first one, because with the first one you go out and think 'Damn! I could have opened it ten metres back!' This is why we usually run two or three sets of qualifiers, depending on what Michelin have bought."

Tyres, riders, engine, chassis and suspension are pushed to the very edge of their performance abilities and sometimes beyond. It requires the most grip, the most feedback, the most perfect lines and the most dedication from the rider to push the limits of physics.

Qualifying is a race but one that lasts for only one lap. It's definitely you against the track, and the rider who does the best job with the track will be on pole. It's as simple as that.

Valentino Rossi works himself hard too: "Yes, I very much talk to myself when I am on the bike. If I brake a little early for a corner and lose some time, I will say to myself 'Fack! Brake a little more deep next time!'"

The idea for qualifying is to build up to that really good lap towards the end of the last session. Now to be fair, at club level you'll be lucky to get ten minutes and your grid position may be no reflection of your time in practice, and more likely decided by your position in the championship and when you got your entry forms in the post and processed!

But as you go up the tree of racing the system becomes fairer and qualifying gets more and more important. Tenths, hundreds or even thousands of a second will become very important – and harder and harder to achieve. Finding one tenth of a second is very hard; losing a whole second is very easy.

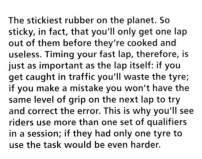

Setting off for the off. You need to decide whether you want to get a tow around for your fast lap or you prefer to have clean and clear space in front of you so that you can do it on your own. Mick Doohan was often quoted as saying that other riders used him as a 'tow truck' to put in one fast lap during qualifying.

The stickiest rubber on the planet. So sticky, in fact, that you'll only get one lap out of them before they're cooked and useless. Timing your fast lap, therefore, is just as important as the lap itself: if you get caught in traffic you'll waste the tyre; if you make a mistake you won't have the same level of grip on the next lap to try and correct the error. This is why you'll see riders use more than one set of qualifiers in a session; if they had only one tyre to use the task would be even harder.

"NORMALLY IN THE RACE YOU RIDE THE BIKE AT 95 PER CENT. IN THE QUALIFYING YOU RIDE THE BIKE AT 110 PER CENT. YOU USE EVERYTHING, ALL THE WHOLE TRACK AND YOU USE THE BIKE REALLY OVER THE LIMIT. YOU LOSE THE FRONT, YOU LOSE THE BACK. ALWAYS YOU ARE OVER THE LIMITS. FOR ME THIS IS VERY GOOD BECAUSE I LIKE TO RIDE THE BIKE THAT WAY."

**LORIS CAPIROSSI**

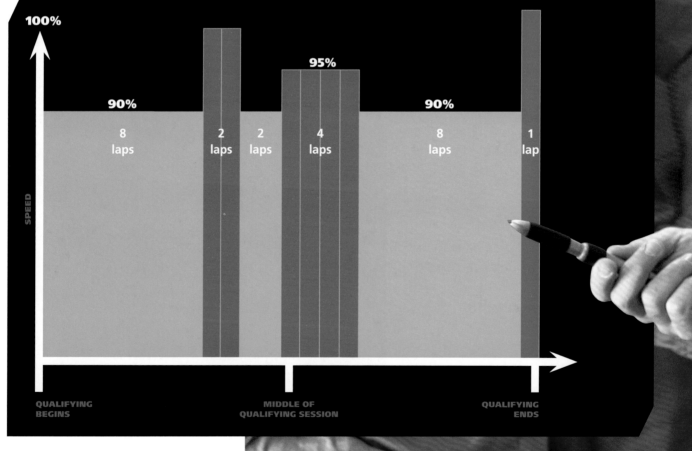

100%

90%

95%

90%

| 8 laps | 2 laps | 2 laps | 4 laps | 8 laps | 1 lap |

SPEED

QUALIFYING BEGINS

MIDDLE OF QUALIFYING SESSION

QUALIFYING ENDS

When a racer goes out in free practice he has two choices: to set up his bike for the race or to set it up for qualifying. A clever rider tries to do both but this isn't always the best plan. If you have a good race set-up but are last on the grid, then it's harder to make up a lot of places. If you have a good qualifying set-up and as a result a good grid position, but your tyres are shot to hell after five laps of the race, then you won't be on the podium. It's a fine balancing act and you'll see a lot of riders only doing two or three fast laps in free practice and one blistering lap in final qualifying. Of course, in MotoGP, with super-sticky qualifying tyres, one lap is all they get before the tyre is useless!

A circuit map of Istanbul Park in Turkey used to help Thomas Lüthi improve his times in each session. Tying up how confident the rider feels in each corner with a read-out of the split times allows me, as a riding coach, to get the best improvements from the rider for the following session and for the upcoming race. Sometimes a rider's confidence will not correlate with what the split times indicate. You have to decide which corners are the most important to get right.

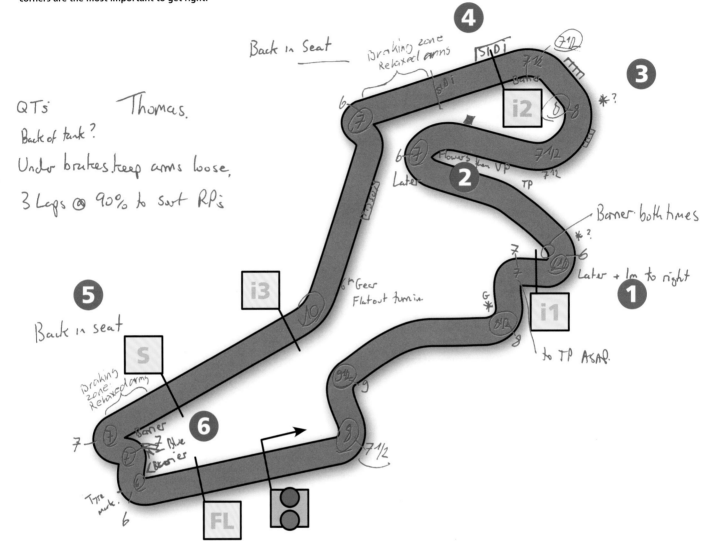

**1** A difficult complex with lots of steep elevation changes and blind approaches. The purpose of the note 'to TP ASAP' is to get Thomas to look for his Turn Point on the last of these corners as soon as he can. He also needs to change his current turning-in point to one that's later and further to the right-hand side. A good plan, but will it work? Will it reduce his times in this section? Or will it be hard to achieve and cause an increase in times?

**2** Turning in later for better drive up the hill. An important part of getting good drive is to know where you are and where you need to go. The flowers on the inside of the turn are a trigger to get him to look further up the track at this point in the corner. Beware, though, that it's possible to look too far ahead. It's a fine balance between creating space and feeling lost.

**3** A question mark in the fastest quadruple apex left-hander in the MotoGP calendar. Thomas wasn't sure where to apex on the second of the four apexes here. A walk around the track gave him some different points to try. Of course, at race speeds some will work and others won't.

**4** The fast downhill approach to this corner can cause riders to lose grip at the front end and crash. It's further complicated by the bumps in the braking area left by F1 cars as they ripple the surface. Having relaxed arms under braking will give the rider more feeling for the front end of the bike and therefore allow him to modulate the brake as required to get the best possible stopping distances the surface and downhill camber will allow.

**5** Braking downhill also moves the rider closer to the back of the fuel tank, making the turn-in point a little more difficult as his arms won't be positioned in a good plane – namely parallel to the surface. By moving back from the tank the arms bend more to help the rider turn the bike more quickly.

**6** The last turn onto the straight and an important one for the final lap. Having a different selection of lines here will allow more options for overtaking on that final lap. If you stick to the one line, how will you know if you can make it better? Again, knowing where you are in the corner gives you the ability to make changes. Some will work, some won't. Better to know early in the weekend.

"YES, I VERY MUCH TALK TO MYSELF WHEN I AM ON THE BIKE. IF I BRAKE A LITTLE EARLY FOR A CORNER AND LOSE SOME TIME, I WILL SAY TO MYSELF 'FACK! BRAKE A LITTLE MORE DEEP NEXT TIME!'"
VALENTINO ROSSI

Shinya Nakano: "I have to move my braking markers in the fast laps for qualifying. With Bridgestone we have an incredible qualifying tyre, but it's only good for one lap. With a race tyre I sometimes have problems with front-end chatter or the bike is difficult to turn in, but with the qualifying tyre all the problems go. You have to adapt the braking points as you want to brake later because of the grip, but sometimes you have to brake in the normal place if you've arrived at the turn much faster, if the tyre has given stronger acceleration because of the extra grip."

This is where a real difference can be made by a suspension or engine mechanic, or by a riding coach. It can make all the difference to have a slight tweak to the suspension so that you can make sure of the extra grip the qualifying tyres give; or to have a slight increase in power lower down the revs so that you can get an extra 1bhp earlier in the corner; or to have been taught to understand how looking into the corner a little earlier will increase your corner entry speed. All these details make a difference, and finding that tenth or two can move you on to the front row.

So, as a rider the pressure is on you to give your crew the best possible feedback. What's the engine doing, how does the front end feel in turn 10, 'I'm feeling lost in turn four' – all this will help your crew to help you go faster. The more you

can communicate, the better. The more accurate your information, the quicker your crew can make a difference to the bike, the tyres, the suspension or you. At the end of the day, qualifying is there to make you go faster, in fact as fast as you and your bike can possibly go!

"Normally in the race you ride the bike at 95 per cent," states Loris Capirossi. "In the qualifying you ride the bike at 110 per cent. You use everything, all the whole track and you use the bike really over the limit. You lose the front, you lose the back. Always you are over the limits. For me this is very good because I like to ride the bike like that way."

Of course, the twist to this is that you'll be riding your socks off, and your ability to read the bike and what you're doing becomes harder the faster you go as you have less and less spare attention. The forces you'll be generating will be huge because you'll be pushing everything harder, including your mental capacity to retain, sample and relive what's going on. You could ride more slowly, but then you're missing the point – and the points at the end of the race.

Nicky Hayden: "With a qualifying tyre I try and make up all my time with the throttle on, braking in the same spot, maybe getting off the brake a little sooner, higher corner speed for when you get to the apex – and then just hit the switch."

Looking over datalogging information can help you work out what's wrong with your bike or what you did wrong in a corner. There's so much information available to a MotoGP rider that working out what's useful and what isn't is an art all in itself. But at the end of the day it'll be down to you, the rider, to work with the bike, the tyres and the team to get the best possible combination.

# STARTING

## Often the short-cut to race victory

Shinya Nakano is really on the money. His head is already tucked down as far behind the screen as he can get it. This will help the bike cut through the air more easily as the speed starts to increase. But how good is his first-corner plan? And will it work and take him to the front?

Reaction times on this grid are awesome. Every single rider, from front to back, is getting off the line and yet the lights must have gone out no more than a tenth of a second before the photo was taken. Casey Stoner has even got both his feet on the pegs already!

Even though he won this race at Le Mans, Marco Melandri is dragging his feet behind. If he doesn't get them on the footpegs soon, the bike will try and wheelie. However, if Honda's launch control is good then it'll restrict the wheelie. The issue then is will it also restrict acceleration?

The starting grid can be a real distraction. There are lots of pretty, scantily clad girls wandering around, mixed in with TV crews, photographers and the noise of the fans in the grandstands. A racer needs to have a plan in his head before he goes to the starting grid and this will help him to cope with all the distractions. Some riders are better at coping than others – and pressure from the media diminishes the further down the grid you go.

Getting your bike off the line is no easy task for several differing reasons. Unless you've been a traffic light junkie or even a quarter-mile freak, the chances are you'll never have practised a good start until the very first time you line up on the grid. At club racing levels you get a ten-minute practice session but never any time to improve your starting techniques. At track days if you were to try starts in the pitlane, paddock or on track, you'd be asked to leave!

I used to load my race bike into the back of my van and go to a straight but deserted country road close to home. Once there I'd get the bike out and spend 30 minutes or so getting it just right. Then back in the van and home. I'll await the summons for that confession.

Colin Edwards tells us that it's all in the clutch feeling. "It's all about the feel in your left hand. Different bikes have different feels; you know, different clutches, dry clutches, wet clutches, that plays a big part in what your feel is. I've been on bikes that I couldn't start to save my life and there's nothing I could do about it. Then you have some bikes where it's impossible to get a bad start because there's a nice smooth release to the clutch – and then you practise. You just have to practise to get that feel."

At the track and on the grid, you'll have the added rush of adrenaline to cope with as you try and get to the first corner in front of the pack. The adrenaline is an assistance because it'll make your reaction times faster, but it'll also have the effect of making you more anxious and more likely to screw up your clutch release or throttle control.

My first race was at Lydden in England in 1994. I'd rented a Yamaha 250LC and as far as I was concerned I was the man. I lined up for my first ever race start about a third of the way down the grid. My heart was pounding as I realised I was racing for the very first time. This was it, the real deal – all the bravado and bullshit that had gone before was about to be tested for real. I watched the flag man intently and as the flag dropped I gave the little 250 its full beans, slipped sideways on the damp surface and nearly took out half the field with my lack of technique. A very memorable start but definitely not what I was looking for!

Getting a good clean start in club racing is where half the battle is won in those short sharp sprint races. I became very good at starts and would always be in the top three or four at the first corner, if not at the front. It was during the later laps that I had problems!

Shinya Nakano: "You should know on your

At the end of each free practice and qualifying session, you'll get the chance to practise your starts. There's normally a pre-defined straight where you'll be able to let loose – make sure you've found out where this is. Getting your feet up and onto the footpegs as soon as the bike starts rolling will help to give you more drive and reduce the chances of an acceleration-sapping wheelie. Dragging the rear brake will also help. Launch control helps too...

PERFORMANCE RIDING TECHNIQUES **115**

bike what's the best rpm – do you start with low or high rpm? And then the clutch – where it bites. Maybe you use a timer – sometimes you think you're faster but it's not always the case. I always check with my datalogger. This may not be possible with your own bike so get someone to time you over a distance."

The basic idea of getting a good start is to get all the drive you can off the line. This means using as much torque as possible from the engine, not the power.

Torque is the twisting motion that an engine producs, and it's this that generates drive. Power, on the other hand, is the force that'll make the bike wheelie and become less controllable – and an excess of power can cause wheelspin and therefore no drive forwards.

But there are several things you can do to make sure that you get your bike off the line quickly and in control. These techniques once helped me to put a nearly stock Suzuki Hayabusa through the standing quarter-mile in 9.98 seconds without having to change tyre pressures or any other quarter-mile trick.

"Always get used to the feeling of the clutch on your bike," recommends Loris Capirossi. "This year we have different parts in our clutch and the starts are harder."

**The starting grid is a busy place. Thankfully it gets thinned out as the time ticks away to the start. This reduces the distractions and allows the rider to get his head in gear and ready for the off. The adrenaline also rises in inverse proportion to the dwindling of the people, and if you haven't got your plan worked out by now then it may be too late...**

**Getting on a MotoGP grid and close to the riders in their environment is no mean task. Fame certainly helps – and fame helps to get the sport on mainstream TV. Brad Pitt, a keen biker and track rider, is seen here on the grid at Laguna Seca. It looks like he made the brolly dolly's day judging by that wry smile!**

## 1 DON'T BLIP

Blipping the throttle doesn't help. When the lights change or the flag drops, you could end up releasing the clutch with the revs in the wrong part of the range for the ideal launch.

## 2 FEED CLUTCH AND THROTTLE

Once you start feeding the clutch out, match it with increasing engine revs so that the load on the engine doesn't make it stall or the revs drop too low, losing you drive. Your goal is to have the clutch out as soon as possible without dropping revs.

## 3 LOOK AT THE TRACK AHEAD

It's very sad to know that most deaths and serious injuries in racing occur on the start/ finish. This is when you're most at risk of colliding with or being collected by another rider. The rules are that if you stall you need to put your hand up as quickly as possible. But if the riders behind have their heads down they won't see you stalled and this is when the problems occur.

As part of my race licence programme that I run in Dubai, starts are one of the areas we cover and practise out on track. Here I make sure that all the racers have their eyes on the track once the lights have changed or the flag has dropped. This way not only is it safer for all the racers on the grid but it also keeps their attention on the track, where it should be as they shoot off towards the first corner.

## 4 USE YOUR EARS

Don't look at the clocks to see what revs you're using as you won't be able to see when the flag drops or the lights change. Use your ears to assess where the bike is revving. If you have to spend time in the paddock learning what the right revs sound like, you'll be able to recognise this on the start line.

## 5 GET YOUR FEET ON THE PEGS

I hate seeing racers trailing their feet behind them as they launch their bikes off the start line. It's not just because it looks untidy – it also prevents the bike from getting away as fast as it could. All that weight dangling at the back of the bike makes it more likely to wheelie and lose speed – more than almost anything else you could do. Getting your feet onto the footpegs as soon as possible moves the weight closer to the centre of mass of the bike, and then all the drive is committed to forward rather than upward motion. And let's face it – one leg should be on the foot rest anyway as you only need one leg to balance the bike at a standstill, not two.

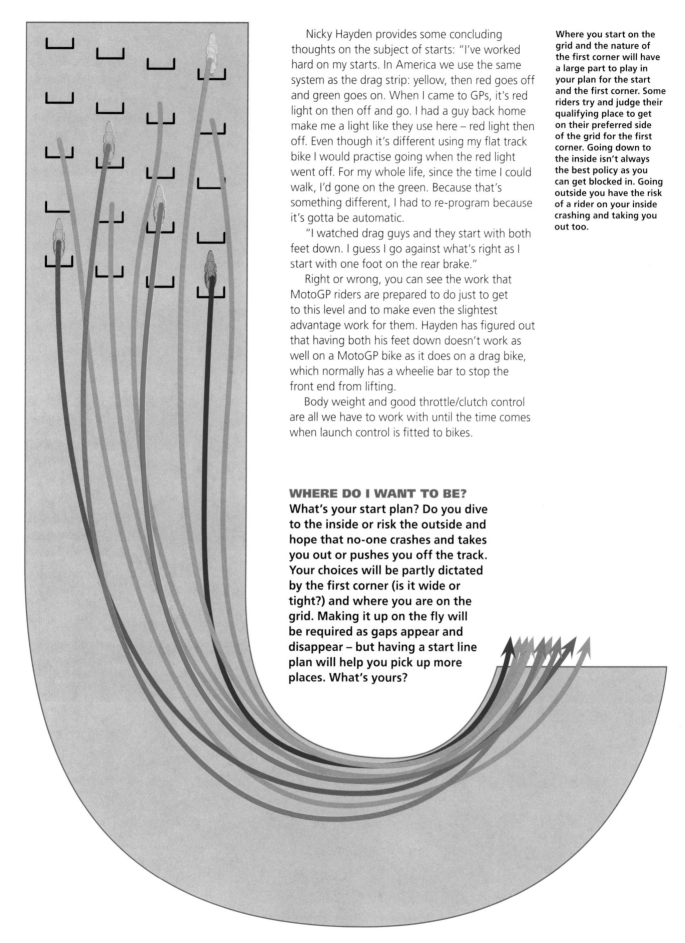

Nicky Hayden provides some concluding thoughts on the subject of starts: "I've worked hard on my starts. In America we use the same system as the drag strip: yellow, then red goes off and green goes on. When I came to GPs, it's red light on then off and go. I had a guy back home make me a light like they use here – red light then off. Even though it's different using my flat track bike I would practise going when the red light went off. For my whole life, since the time I could walk, I'd gone on the green. Because that's something different, I had to re-program because it's gotta be automatic.

"I watched drag guys and they start with both feet down. I guess I go against what's right as I start with one foot on the rear brake."

Right or wrong, you can see the work that MotoGP riders are prepared to do just to get to this level and to make even the slightest advantage work for them. Hayden has figured out that having both his feet down doesn't work as well on a MotoGP bike as it does on a drag bike, which normally has a wheelie bar to stop the front end from lifting.

Body weight and good throttle/clutch control are all we have to work with until the time comes when launch control is fitted to bikes.

Where you start on the grid and the nature of the first corner will have a large part to play in your plan for the start and the first corner. Some riders try and judge their qualifying place to get on their preferred side of the grid for the first corner. Going down to the inside isn't always the best policy as you can get blocked in. Going outside you have the risk of a rider on your inside crashing and taking you out too.

**WHERE DO I WANT TO BE?**
**What's your start plan? Do you dive to the inside or risk the outside and hope that no-one crashes and takes you out or pushes you off the track. Your choices will be partly dictated by the first corner (is it wide or tight?) and where you are on the grid. Making it up on the fly will be required as gaps appear and disappear – but having a start line plan will help you pick up more places. What's yours?**

First turn at Catalunya. Because of the width of the track and the distance from the start line to the first corner, you can get up a lot of speed here. The better you can get off the line, the more options will open up to you as you get closer to the first turn, as seen here.

# OVERTAKING

Ways and means of
making it to the front

James Ellison and Valentino Rossi. The Italian is about to overtake the British rider on the outside of the turn. He has gone into the corner with more speed, maybe even too much speed, as he's still braking while Ellison is off the brake at this point. Both riders are looking where they want to go next, but it's Rossi who has got there first.

"IT'S IMPOSSIBLE FOR US TO
OVERTAKE ON THE POWER,
IT'S DEFINITELY BRAKING.
EVEN IF I HAD THE
HORSEPOWER IT WOULD
STILL BE UNDER BRAKING."
JOHN HOPKINS

There are five ways to overtake other riders on tracks. They can be smooth and clean, they can be a little risky, they can be wild and they can be damned unsporting old boy!

We can pass riders on the way into a corner or pass on the way out. We can bump another rider off line or use ungentlemanly throttle control to force them to take avoiding action, and finally we can fake-brake them.

The sheer satisfaction of a good overtaking manoeuvre in a race is hard to beat. It's the one real defining moment of the race track and racing. And the better you are at it the more scalps you can claim.

Now, there are two types of overtaking: those you can do on a track day and those you can use in racing. I make the distinction as many track day riders, namely *leisure* riders, have a totally wrong idea of what a good overtake is on a track day.

On a track day you really do need to consider your fellow track dayer. Most track dayers are there to push themselves and their bikes a certain

# THE FIVE WAYS TO PASS IN A RACE

**1 ON THE WAY IN**

**2 ON THE WAY OUT**

**3 BUMPING**

**4 UNGENTLEMANLY THROTTLE CONTROL**

**5 FAKE BRAKING**

amount, but with a degree of caution. They're not racing. In fact most organisers will ensure there's no hint of racing as it voids their insurance, and it's dangerous because most of the other riders aren't racing. If you really do think you're that good, then do the real thing!

Most track day riders are there to have fun and push harder than they can do safely or legally on the road – and then go home in one piece.

So, stuffing it up the inside of someone who's just turning in is a legitimate strategy in racing but an absolute no-no on a track day.

The risk to you and the other rider is too great for a leisure pursuit. It can spook riders into never going on the track again. It might make you think you're Valentino Rossi but everyone else will think you're something entirely different.

There are several overtaking options open to the track day rider and the racer alike depending on the level of the playing field. Some options are more acceptable to one type of day than the other and vice versa.

Is your overtaking plan a good and considered one or is it one that's full of risk and derring-do? A lot of places can be made up in the first corner of a race but the chances of crashing are much greater due to the sheer number of riders all trying to use the same piece of track as you. No-one wants to lose a place in the first corner and everyone's trying to make up at least one place. It's a risky time.

As we have already seen, overtaking on the way into the corner is the method with the most risk on a track day, and this is mainly due to ignorance. Most riders who come to the track have been used to road riding, where most of the overtaking is done on the straights. It's rare to be duffed up on the inside as you turn in on a public road. This is mainly due to the fact that road users won't, on the whole, try this kind of manoeuvre, and normally a biker would be riding with mates with the same mindset of having some fun riding in a group and not racing each other.

But on the track during a race, the gloves are off and he who is in front is the one who gets more points and pots.

There's another important point to consider here. Racers *do* expect undertaking to happen and as such are much more aware of the chances of this occurring and more comfortable with the lack of space it creates. In fact, 'rubbing's racing' and contact is neither a shock nor surprise unless it creates a crash. Ask Valentino Rossi after the first race of the 2006 season when Toni Elias clouted him in the rear at the first corner and the multiple World Champion ended up on the deck. While contact is expected, there's also a respect between riders that gets deeper the further up the field you go.

Rossi said of that incident: "I saw Toni come up on the inside and he hit me; this is racing and these things happen. I have known Toni for many years and he is a good rider. He apologised to me after the race so I told him not to worry – only to remember to brake next time and if it is too late then to hit another bike instead of me!"

There are two important things to be learned from this quote.

Firstly, always apologise to the rider you hit whether he went down or not. A race paddock is a close-knit environment and everyone is expected to be fair and respect each other.

Secondly, there needs to be a degree of trust between all of the riders, and if people judge you to be a loose cannon then you'll be classed as a dangerous rider and the doors of the paddock will slowly close on you. Even worse, you could be banned from racing if the club or racing body considers you a danger to other riders.

An experienced racer will also have a better idea of when to lean on the other rider, or close the door on him, or give it up. He has been there, had it done to him, and knows how to ride in a tight pack. The first time a track dayer races, he can get a bit of a shock on this point alone. On a track day it's not expected, it's not needed, it's out of order – and it can cause a crash and injury.

**1** If you leave the door open, any racer who's close enough will take the invitation with open arms. The real question here is this: do you want to give up the place, a safe tactic, or are you willing to close the door on the other rider?

**2** Once the rider on the inside has a wheel in front of you, there's little you can do about it as any manoeuvre now is likely to have both of you off and into the gravel trap.

**3** The best plan is to get behind the other rider and see if you can out-drive him on the exit of the corner. If he has gone into the corner too early, he'll be unable to get on the throttle as hard as you on the exit, giving you a chance to re-pass. Of course, if he blocks you, then you'll have to roll off the throttle slightly to avoid a possible collision and therefore not be able to make up the ground in that corner.

**1** One of the most controversial overtakes of MotoGP history took place at Jerez, Spain, in 2005. Valentino Rossi enters the corner on the inside and with a lot of speed. Sete Gibernau comes in on his more conventional line. A few years earlier, Mick Doohan and Alex Criville had a similar incident at this corner – the final hairpin on to the start/finish line – on 500cc GP bikes.

**2** Neck and neck. Can Gibernau see Rossi? Probably not at this stage, but he sure as hell would have heard his bike. It's the last corner of the last lap. Would you give it up?

**3** Gibernau is still on his chosen line but Rossi is now looking for a piece of that line too – and he's fast running out of room.

**4** Side by side. Rossi isn't concerned if they collide. This is clear because he isn't looking anywhere else except at the piece of track he wants. Gibernau is just as focused. With neither rider wanting to give an inch, there's only one possible result from this...

**5** ...collision. The two riders slam into each other as neither wanted to give it up to the other. Was Rossi too aggressive? Was Gibernau too bloody-minded? Both riders could have ended up on the floor and neither of them would have scored points. It was a high-risk strategy by both of them.

To overtake on the inside you have to weigh up the risks and compromises you'll face. You'll be off line on the way in. You won't be able to get on the throttle as quickly or as hard as you can when you are on line. You might get the door well and truly shut in your face, and when that happens contact and crashing can occur. Do you have the room to make the move? Will the other rider give it up or take no prisoners? This is where the mind games in the paddock could bear fruit.

The rider you're undertaking might not be keen to give it up and lean on you to get you to back off – will you be able to weigh up the risks in the white-hot heat of racing?

In MotoGP this is the only real overtaking technique you can use.

"It's impossible for us to overtake on the power, it's definitely braking," says John Hopkins. "Even if I had the horsepower it would still be under braking."

Unless the rider in front gets it really wrong, the chances of you overtaking on the way out are slim or even non-existent. And outbraking on the way in will be difficult too. All the riders in MotoGP are the best in the world. All of them have come up through the ranks and know what to expect and what to do in response.

Overtaking on the way out is a much better, safer tactic on a track day but it'll be nearly

impossible the higher you go up the racing tree. On a track day you can pretty much guarantee that the rider you have lined up will go all the way to the outside of the corner on the exit, provided the corner leads on to a straight. So staying to the outside for longer on the entry will allow you to drive underneath him on the way out. This is a lot cleaner, safer and more predictable than overtaking on the way in.

As a racer, overtaking on the exit gets harder to do because you'll want to use all the track as you're going fast. The gap in ability also gets smaller the higher you go. A MotoGP rider running in 20th place isn't slow and will get on the gas just as hard as you on the exit. This makes the technique less likely to be used in a race unless you have a big power advantage.

Bumping someone off line in the corner is another tactic, but again only reserved for racing and even then it's considered a little hard and ungentlemanly. This didn't stop Rossi doing it to Sete Gibernau in the last turn at Jerez in the first GP of 2005. For a lot of people, Sete included, this was the defining moment of the season, and it simply destroyed Sete's determination to win. Gibernau had the ability in him – he set a lot of fastest laps and pole positions – but he didn't want to mix it that badly in the rest of the races that season. As a result there was very little to

challenge Rossi as he secured yet another World Championship MotoGP title.

The tactic also carries a high degree of risk. Rossi could have just as easily crashed himself during the contact. As the turn was a left-hander, his front brake lever could have become snagged and one or both of them could have hit the deck.

Another ungentlemanly method is to check the throttle halfway through a corner. This will get you in front, and it can give you a few bike lengths on the exit of a turn. When you get

**Sete Gibernau came out worse. Luckily neither rider was seriously hurt and neither rider crashed. This is best described as a racing incident as you should be willing to take risks to win races. It's great when they pay off, but when they don't there shouldn't be an issue as long as no-one is hurt. In this case the mental victory Rossi had over Gibernau could be classed as the defining moment for that season – Sete wasn't prepared to play that hard.**

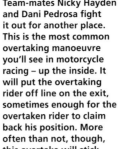

Team-mates Nicky Hayden and Dani Pedrosa fight it out for another place. This is the most common overtaking manoeuvre you'll see in motorcycle racing – up the inside. It will put the overtaking rider off line on the exit, sometimes enough for the overtaken rider to claim back his position. More often than not, though, this overtake will stick.

mid-corner you roll off the throttle slightly, forcing the guy behind to take some form of avoiding action –rolling out of the throttle, sitting the bike up and going off line, or touching the brakes. While he's doing any one or more of these things, you can get back on the gas and pull a few lengths on him at the exit of the turn. This works really well in a slow, hairpin-type corner as the effect is much greater than in a fast one.

The final way to overtake is to outbrake your opponent. This will mean that you'll have to dive down the inside at the entry of the turn. However, if you could outbrake him from the outside of the turn you'd still get in front but have to chop his nose off as you turned in – a cheeky way to get in front but valid nonetheless.

Outbraking means you'll lose some mid-corner speed and this is why there's a greater chance of getting re-passed on the exit of the turn. Leaving your braking later creates more forces (see the *Braking* chapter) which will lower your entry speed or conversely put you into the corner faster but unable to get back on the throttle.

Sitting it out on the brakes with another rider is excellent fun, but don't forget there's a corner coming! I fell foul of this one day at Snetterton defending my position on the back straight. I was getting hassle from another rider so I looked ahead and saw a slower rider – it was the last lap so my plan was to put him between us. I was so intent on getting past the rider in front that when the 100-metre board flashed past in the corner of my eye I was still prone and pinned. I knew I was in trouble – I would normally have braked at the 200-metre board.

Another way is to trick the other rider into thinking you've braked when you haven't. With the other rider next to you, sit up at your normal braking point – but wait a bit before hitting the brakes. The other rider will assume you're braking because you've sat up – and he'll brake first. As you tend to get into the habit of braking as you pop up, you should practise different sequences to outwit your fellow racers.

I was once in a dyno room with Kevin Schwantz watching from outside. I revved the bike we had on test through the box to full revs in top and then rolled out the throttle to slow it down at the end of the run. I looked over to see Schwantz doubled up laughing. Great. I must have done something to make myself look stupid in front of one of the greatest riders ever.

When I got outside the dyno room he came over, still laughing.

"Hey man, you did the same thing I did," he said as he wiped the tears from his eyes. "You rolled off and grabbed the front brake. Where's the bike going to go?"

Bastard.

Many novice racers overtake whenever any opportunities arise. This isn't always a wise plan, particularly in a series of turns where your gain in one corner can be lost in the next. Unless your overtaking is a surefire thing because you're significantly faster than the rider in front, it'll require a bit of planning.

The example we see here is of a rider who's too keen to get up the inside and not considering the result of the second corner. All the overtaken rider has to do is hold his line and he'll overtake at the end of the second corner without any risk or drama.

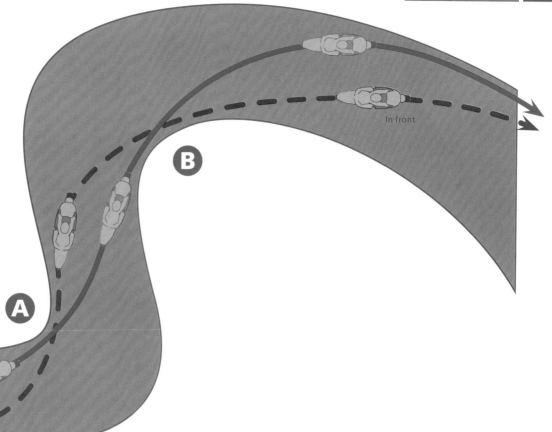

# OUTWITTING

Learn how to out-psyche the opposition, and how others have famously done so

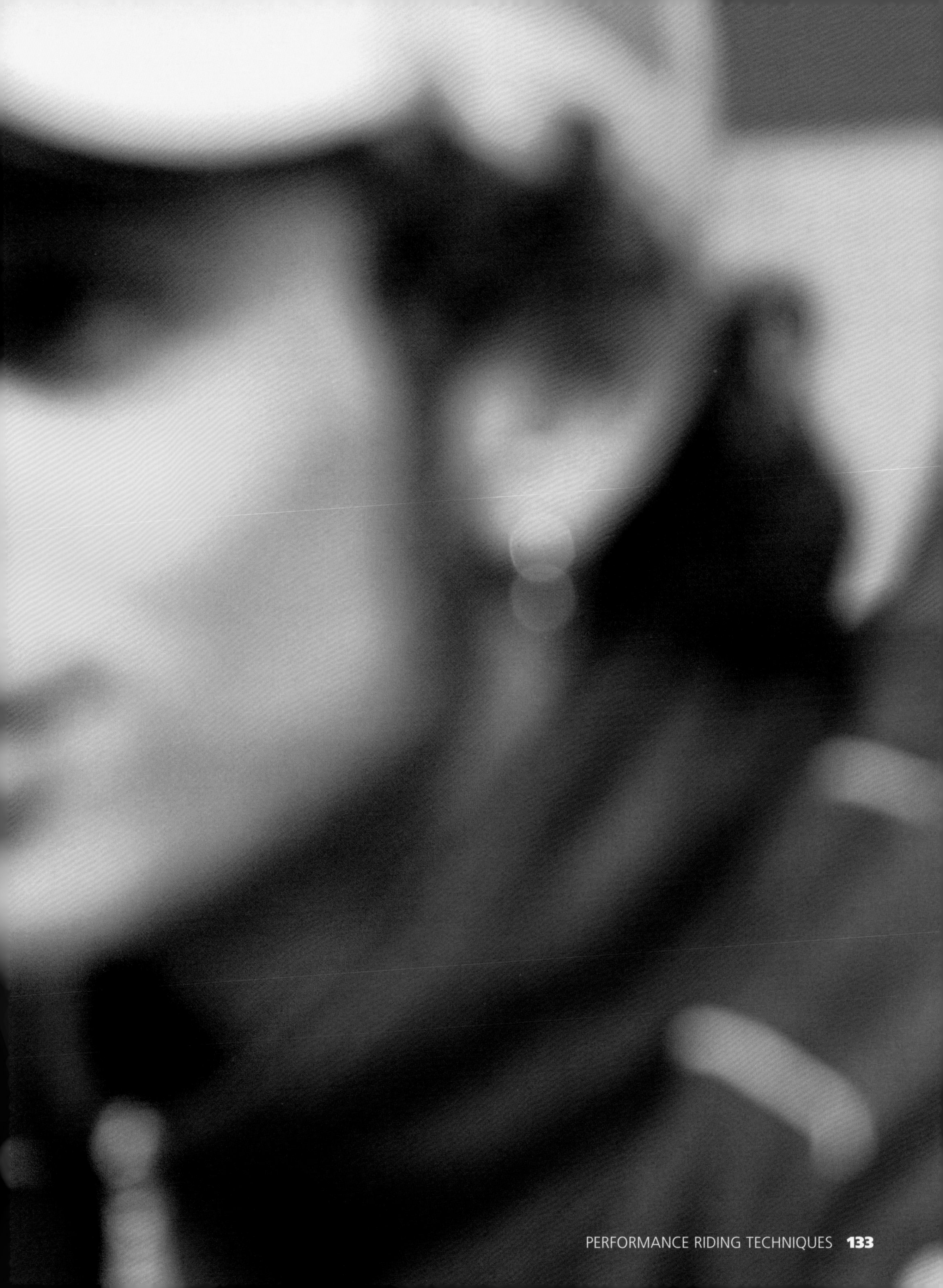

Colin Edwards and John Hopkins chewing the fat – or so it might seem. As they ride for different teams, it's likely that they're trying to find out what the other has planned for the race. What tyres will they run? What's the start plan? Is there one place where the other rider is weak? Or strong? Playing mind games in the paddock can be just as important as the racing on the day...

Once you get on to the racing tree and climb higher up the branches, particularly at national level where everyone literally speaks the same language, the use of mind games becomes quite an art form. Riders use fair and sometimes foul means of putting their rivals off balance, whether in the paddock, in the run-up to a race, on the grid or in the race itself.

Niall Mackenzie once confessed to me that he used to go around the other riders asking how they were dealing with the 'bump' in turn such and such. He'd tell them that his bike was struggling in that turn and ask for help. In reality there was no bump and the corner was one of his best, but other riders soon started to develop the same 'problem'. Out on track at the corner in question, he'd then start to see other riders encountering problems with their bike set-up and as a result overtake in the most bizarre places...

John Hopkins has this to say: "Mind games are all part of the whole deal, whether it be killing them with kindness or mind games with their heads – it's all part of it. I used to have a team-mate in America and when he first came to the team he was always worrying about lap times. Every time he got off the bike he would come over and ask me what my lap times were. Once he asked

me in the middle of a session: I bullshitted him and told him a time that was just ridiculous, but he went off and tried to match it. He must have run off the track eight times. Luckily he didn't crash and came in at the end of the session and saw my real times and said – 'what the hell!'"

James Ellison is another current MotoGP rider with a confession from days of old: "Sometimes I used to tell other riders I had a certain tyre on when I didn't."

Wayne Rainey used to slide the bike when in front of other riders as if to say: 'Look at me. I'm in total control and perfectly happy with the bike being out of shape – can you do this?'

Some riders will really go to extremes to try and upset their opponents. Kevin Schwantz once asked Wayne Rainey's sister out on a date just to mess with Rainey's head...

A brilliant mind game I once witnessed concerned a club racer who decided he'd pretend at the first corner that he'd lost control and was about to crash. Before the race he confided that he'd take to the grass on the inside and pretend to be out of control by waving his legs about and moving the bike around underneath him. Come the race, everyone started, he did his stunt and all the riders behind, without exception, backed off as they thought he was going to skittle them

"SOMETIMES I USED TO
TELL OTHER RIDERS I
HAD A CERTAIN TYRE
ON WHEN I DIDN'T."
**JAMES ELLISON**

In the wet at Donington Park, July 2005. Rossi comes across the line with a massive lead. In the rain he started slowly and built his understanding of where there was traction and where there wasn't – until he had the track figured out. Then he went on to set the fastest lap and pulled away from everyone else by a staggering second or more a lap. He destroyed the opposition – this would have had a hugely demoralising effect on the other riders. His violin-playing as he crossed the line told the other riders whose tune they were playing too.

all in his crash – and he ended up with a massive lead on the first lap!

Examples are endless, but the most important thing is to pick on something that other riders will feel uncomfortable with.

Other tactics include and aren't restricted to:

- Hiding gloves or earplugs.
- Going into another rider's motorhome when you know he's preparing mentally.
- Telling other riders you're really struggling when you're not.
- Giving false gearing advice.
- Telling another rider your race set-up when you don't actually have one.
- Saying you're planning to use one type of tyre for the race and then using something else.
- Giving friendly advice that's wrong, on subjects such as braking points, turn-in points or lines.

Luckily for any rider at club level, at the grass roots of racing, the paddock is like one great big social club, and all the riders there will help out newcomers as they join the field of battle. It's unlikely that you'll be stitched up by another rider unless, of course, he's battling with you for the lead of the championship. In that case be careful, and take all 'advice' with a big pinch of salt.

If you're a seasoned club racer, you should make it your job to look out for new riders and help them as much as possible. After all, they're the new talent coming into the frame, and one day you could be having the race of your life with them and be pleased it's such good fun to find another opponent who can give you a challenge.

This could well be the reason why Valentino Rossi has tested Formula One cars and has even considered a move to four wheels instead of staying to compete on bikes. However, with the challenge of the new young generation arriving and winning races straight away, it looks like he'll stay on in the sport a little longer.

**When a rider sits up (left), does it really mean he has started his braking? It's a great manoeuvre to use if you're duking it out on the brakes with another racer. If you sit up but don't touch the brakes, I guarantee that the other rider will assume you've hit the brakes and dive on his, allowing you to gain that vital bike length to get in front. Remember, though, that this technique will require that you sit up *before* your normal marker. Don't worry about this: the other rider will be concentrating on you so much that he'll just react to you sitting up rather than his own braking marker!**

# CRASHING

## How to minimise the risks of coming to grief

It happens to the best in the world. Crashing is something you have to accept if you race – it's likely to happen at some stage. Casey Stoner's answer to the problem is to surf his bike into the gravel! A nice trick if you can get away with it, but usually you end up eating dirt. Having crash bungs on your bike will reduce the amount of damage you have to repair after an off.

Valentino Rossi testing the gravel trap. It's not seen very often, but even The Doctor can push a little too far and make a mistake. Luckily, thanks to the nature of the tracks and the quality of the riding kit he wears, the chances of injury are reduced.

**There comes a point when you need to let go of the bike before its weight drags you into more trouble. When a bike and rider get mixed up in a crash, the chances of getting hurt are greatly increased. Racers often talk about kicking the bike away from them: whether or not that's possible, the idea is sound.**

OK, first things first. It *will* happen. One very memorable advert, for a helmet manufacturer, shows Max Biaggi midway through a full-on highside from a 500cc Yamaha with a caption stating, 'Even our heroes make mistakes'.

One of the things we must take on the chin when we make the choice to ride a bike is the fact that we could crash and get hurt or even killed. It's one of the risks of riding – and it makes us feel alive.

Your mindset about crashing is one of the first things you'll have to tackle. You should be prepared that it's going to happen one day and accept that. If you spend your entire riding career thinking 'I don't want to fall, I don't want to fall', you'll be constantly distracted from the job in hand – riding the bike – and you'll make a mistake because your concentration is in the wrong place. And you'll fall.

Accept it for what it is, particularly on the track, as you'll be riding harder and cornering faster, and asking more of yourself, your bike and your tyres.

The advantage of being on the track rather than the road is that you can make these intense demands with impunity. There are fewer things for you to hit. There are fewer distractions.

There are no cars coming the other way. And on most circuits you're pretty much guaranteed medical cover within minutes rather than hours.

"If I'm going to crash then the first thing I try and do is stay on the track," says Thomas Lüthi.

"When you make a mistake that means you are too fast," says Loris Capirossi. "It's better to pick up the bike and go in the gravel because normally on these tracks we have space."

All of these aspects allow you to ride that little bit harder than on the street. You can be more committed and with that comes a greater, if somewhat safer, risk.

But there are many things you can do to reduce risk. Many of these have been covered in the *Conserving* chapter, but here are some more crash-focused points.

Let's take a look at the factors that cause crashes and the types of crash we're most likely to face on the track.

**1** Too much lean angle? Is that possible on a MotoGP bike with the best rubber on the rims – rubber you can't even buy? Well, yes, it's possible to lean a MotoGP bike over too far and ask too much of the traction you have at hand.

**2** No sign of danger yet other than the fact that Rossi's elbow is getting very close to the floor. But to be fair this is normal at this level of racing. Thomas Lüthi has been known to drag his elbow on a kerb in the 125 class – with skinny tyres.

**3** Now we know there's something amiss. With his outside leg off the footpeg and, more importantly, off the tank as well, all his body weight is transferring to his inside knee and the handlebars. From this point it's difficult, if not impossible, to save.

**4** But he keeps on trying. Unlike most lowside crashes, it looks as if both tyres have let go at exactly the same moment. Normally the rear starts to come around in this type of incident.

**5** Beyond the point of return. Even good throttle control cannot save this one. The best plan of action now is to let the bike go and slide across the track with plenty of your body's surface area on the ground to help you to slow down as quickly as possible.

## THE LOWSIDE

Of the two categories of crash, the lowside is the less painful on you and your wallet. A lowside happens when you lose front tyre adhesion and the bike, which will already be leant over, simply falls to the ground and slides.

### Causes

Overuse of the front brake while leant over. This is very common in racing as riders trail the brake into the corner and to the apex before they get back on the throttle to balance the bike.

Too much lean angle for the conditions. Normally this occurs in the wet but it can also happen in the dry. On a production bike you could lean it over too far and drag one of the parts of the bike on the ground, causing the weight to be lifted off the tyres – and down you go.

Too much lean with a closed throttle, thus putting excessive weight on the front tyre. This is common on track days and normally happens when the rider goes into the corner at a speed that far outweighs his ability – charging the turn. A frantic late-braking manoeuvre is great preparation for a crash.

Running off the tyre with too much lean. This is rare but can still happen. The rear will normally break away first but the bike will still go down on the low side.

Lifting the front tyre off the ground by scraping too much is common on hairpins – and roundabouts.

"RELAX. RELAX YOUR
BODY AND WAIT.
WAIT TO SEE WHAT
HAPPENS."
**LORIS CAPIROSSI**

## THE HIGHSIDE

This is when the rear tyre breaks traction and then regains grip suddenly. The suspension compresses and then unloads very quickly, effectively catapulting the rider over the highest side of the bike – hence the name. It's very sudden and in most cases very painful, as it's much the same as jumping out your bedroom window and landing on your head and shoulder. Avoid at all costs!

### Causes

The most common cause of this kind of crash is too much throttle, causing the rear to slide, followed by sudden closing of the throttle when the rider feels that the back of the bike has stepped out of line too much with the front.

Too much lean over a surface change: this is more common on the road but can still happen on the track as a lot of circuits don't have as perfect a surface as you'd expect, particularly those tracks that have are used by a lot of race cars – they ripple the surface badly as they generate higher forces under braking.

Lifting the rear tyre off the ground by scraping too much: even with rear sets that raise the height of the footpegs, you can still scrape them – or another part of the bike – on the floor, lightening the load on the tyres and causing loss of traction.

The rear tyre heating up as it spins until the temperature makes it grip suddenly: this isn't very common, but happens when a rider likes to slide the rear of the bike. When it does happen, it's usually with a road-type tyre being used on track.

"If you highside it's not so easy to do something," states Shinya Nakano. "But if you try to do too many things you can tumble and get hurt, so I try to slide."

When your crash happens, you need to reduce the chances of injury as much as possible given the situation you find yourself in. There's a great section in Keith Code's *Twist of the Wrist* DVD where he talks about relaxing when you get thrown off your bike. To illustrate this he gives a drill whereby you practise letting your body go completely limp and fall to the ground.

John Hopkins backs this up: "Go with the flow. As I go down I try and ease my fall with my elbow. As long as I'm on the tarmac I try and put as much leather on the ground as possible to slow myself down and to keep myself as level as possible until I hit the gravel. Once I hit the gravel, if one of my limbs catches then again I go with the flow and try and tumble as little as possible."

"Relax. Relax your body and wait. Wait to see what happens," advises Loris Capirossi.

I've seen similar ideals in some martial arts and it does take a lot of practice to relax as your natural reaction is to brace for impact!

Valentino Rossi testing the limits of traction to the extreme at Donington Park in 2005. As the bike gets too far sideways (even for him), he has no choice but to check the throttle. As the back end de-compresses, he's sent into the air. Luckily for him his outside (left) leg is still in contact with the bike at the highest point of his ejection. This allowed him to land back on the bike when gravity finally took a hold. No, he didn't fall, and went on to win the race by a staggering margin.

Yes, man *can* fly. Marco Melandri comes to grief at the end of a corner. Having highsided, he now has to relax himself for the forthcoming impact. Hopefully by the time he lands the bike will have moved out of the way and therefore reduce the chances of injury. The rider can help this situation in advance by having good-quality riding kit. Boots, helmet, gloves, back protectors: every little thing will help and you'll be glad of the investment you made.

"I just kind of tense everything up," says James Ellison. "Your muscles will protect you more than your bones will. If you tense everything up it's like a cushion."

Better than that, Keith Code once told me while I was still racing that you should count to ten after you've fallen off as you sometimes try to stand up when you're still sliding along at 30mph. I applied this in a crash at Brands Hatch when I found myself sliding along watching my bike destroy itself next to me. When I thought I'd come to a stop, I started to count to ten. I got to eight when I hit the steel barrier at about 20mph. Yes, it did hurt. I can still clearly recall seeing a marshal's head appear over the barrier to ask if I was all right.

Chris Vermeulen agrees: "Wait until you've stopped before you try to get up. What I do is wait until I've almost come to a stop and then put my hand on the ground to make sure I've definitely stopped. Sometimes you think you've stopped and start to get up – and end up trying to do 30-metre steps!"

It's also quite easy to become disoriented and end up running to the inside of the track across the flow of traffic to safety, only to discover you were a stride away from the outside of the track!

But before you make a move, check how much traffic is around. If you just leap up and make a run for it, you'll make it much harder for other riders to avoid you because you're moving. It also increases the chances of them target-fixing on you and hitting you anyway. A stationary hazard is easier to avoid that a moving one!

### PROTECTION

Wearing the right kit, of course, will also help reduce the chances of injury and you should never skimp on your clothing. Your crash helmet should be the best you can afford – after all, how much is your head worth? And remember once again that crashing is a matter of when, not if. Helmet design has changed very little over the years, but the use of lighter and stronger materials has helped to give the rider much more protection. The lighter the helmet, the less effect it has if your head is flicked from one side to the other, thus saving possible neck injuries as you fall and come into contact with asphalt, gravel, grass and possibly your bike.

The same goes for boots. These are rarely made of leather nowadays as various plastics and other materials allow boot designers and manufacturers much more inventiveness in devising protection for the foot, ankle and lower leg.

Leathers are a slightly different matter. For a racer, leathers that offer good protection but will need to go in the bin after one crash are probably not a good option unless you're sponsored, as Colin

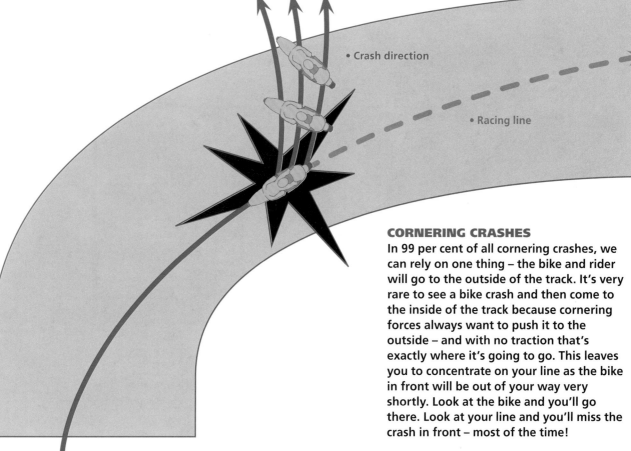

• Crash direction

• Racing line

### CORNERING CRASHES

In 99 per cent of all cornering crashes, we can rely on one thing – the bike and rider will go to the outside of the track. It's very rare to see a bike crash and then come to the inside of the track because cornering forces always want to push it to the outside – and with no traction that's exactly where it's going to go. This leaves you to concentrate on your line as the bike in front will be out of your way very shortly. Look at the bike and you'll go there. Look at your line and you'll miss the crash in front – most of the time!

- **RELAX, SPREAD OUT, CREATE A LARGE SURFACE AREA**
- **COUNT TO TEN**
- **GET ORIENTATED BEFORE YOU MOVE**
- **KEEP STILL IF THERE'S TRAFFIC AROUND**
- **IF YOU HAVE CRASH BUNGS OR RACE BODYWORK – FIT IT!**

Edwards proves: "It's almost natural now, just a reflex. I try and stay on my ass and just slide. If I'm tumbling then it's all assholes and elbows and you don't really know where you're going to end up except in a yard sale with your boots, gloves and leathers!"

Leathers that can handle several offs before needing repair but still offer good protection are better suited (ha, ha!) to the club racer. A track day rider might be happier with the saves-your-skin-but-goes-in-the-bin variety since his plan isn't to come off so often as his risk level is slightly lower than the racer's. Racers will push it and track day riders won't, at least not to the same level – and if they do they should be racing anyway.

The style and protection levels of race leathers have moved on over the years and the current favourite choice of hide is kangaroo. This has the same properties as cow hide but is significantly lighter, allowing the rider to move around on his bike more easily – this in itself is a good safety point. And although there are other more high-tech materials on the market, leather still offers the best resistance to heat and

therefore burns are less of a problem if you're sliding down the track at over 100mph. There's also the addition of body armour, hard and soft, to further protect you in the event of a fall. Titanium and plastic cups on the outside of the shoulders also add additional impact and sliding protection.

Gloves are harder to sort out. Even in this day and age, with lots of different materials available to manufacturers, the hands are hard to protect without loss of feel and feedback because of their physical complexity and dexterity. Any design of glove will be a compromise and you have to decide which design is best for you. More feel means better control and in theory fewer crashes. But crashes *will* happen. Have I said that already?

Finally, get a back protector and make it a

good one. A back protector is not compulsory but highly advisable – I can vouch for that as my back was broken in a racing accident when I was run over. And that was *with* a back protector. The doctors at the hospital told me that I wouldn't be walking now if I hadn't been wearing it. So, get one! And if you're using the excuse that it's uncomfortable, then you've just got the wrong one. Spend some time trying different makes and types until you find one that does fit comfortably. You need to be in a

riding position to tell if it's right or wrong – it's no good standing up straight in the shop without your leathers on.

The back protector was claimed to be invented by racing legend Barry Sheene, who cobbled together a system with old visors. This allowed his back to bend one way but stopped it from bending the other. This design was given to Italian racing leathers manufacturer Dainese, who then developed it into one of the types we see today with a hard carapace spine.

Since then the materials available to use for impact absorption have improved and there are several different types of back protector on the market, but basically they fall into two categories: those with hard armour and those without. Which you choose is up to you, but either is better than none at all.

Steer clear of the light foam back protectors that come fitted into some sets of leathers. They'll feel more comfortable but won't really offer the same level of protection as those designed specifically for the job. However, some manufacturers do offer good back protectors fitted to some of their suits.

Hopefully back protectors will become compulsory for all track days and races in the near future – at the moment, incredibly, they're just a recommendation.

**THE RULES**

**When you go racing the rules are a little more stringent. Here are the 2006 regulations for MotoGP as taken from the FIM road racing handbook.**

■ Riders must wear a complete leather suit with additional leather padding or other protection on the principal contact points, knees, elbows, hips, shoulders, etc.

■ Linings or undergarments must not be made of a synthetic material which might melt and cause damage to the rider's skin.

■ Riders must wear leather gloves and boots.

■ Leather substitute materials may be used if checked by the Chief Technical Scrutineer.

■ Use of a back protector is highly recommended (*author's note: this is ridiculous – back protectors should be compulsory at all racing and track events*).

■ Helmets must be full-faced and of one of the following standards:
  ● EU – ECE20-04 and ECE 22-05P
  ● Japan – JIST 8133:2000
  ● USA – Snell M2005
  ● Visors must be shatterproof

# CLIMATE CONTROL

## Special techniques appropriate to extremes of heat, cold and wet

Riding in the wet with over 250bhp has as many issues in a straight line as when the bike is leant over. With this amount of power you have to be really careful with the throttle as the tyre will spin even if it's a full racing wet. As the tyre spins you lose drive and therefore time. It's also important to make sure that you're warm, if not dry. Boots with venting probably aren't the best choice.

In the extreme heat of somewhere like Losail in Qatar you need to do everything you can to keep as cool as possible. Venting in your leathers will help to keep wind flowing around your body, but when the air temperature is over 100 degrees you'll still be quite hot by the end of a session.

A good racer can do it all in all conditions. It's a sure sign that someone has a good grasp of all the basic, foundation skills if he can ride to a high standard in the wet, in the dry, in the wind, in the calm, in the heat and in the cold. A racer who can handle all of these conditions is most likely to be the championship winner at the end of the season.

There are riders who shine in less favourable conditions: when the weather is overcast, when rain is falling or when it's too damned cold to get any heat in the tyres.

And it's all there for you to learn. Early in their careers, Niall Mackenzie, Randy Mamola and even Valentino Rossi were all terrible in wet conditions, but all three learned the subtleties of the bike, its set-up and how to ride it as the heavens opened. As a result they all have an advantage, not a disadvantage, when conditions change for the 'worse'. Worse for whom? The other riders of course!

Riding in the rain is one of the most rewarding and satisfying ways of improving your own natural ability to control the amount of traction you have and feel.

Most of us shy away from riding in the wet. It's cold and no fun, and your fear of lobbing it up the track is much higher than when blasting along in the dry.

Out on the track the benefits to be had are huge – the biggest one being a better understanding of traction limits.

Now, like most things we do on a bike, the natural reactions we have in the wet go exactly against what we need – to have good control over our bike in conditions of reduced grip.

Here are some things we do:

Tense up.

Delay throttle application.

Target-fix on the places we don't want the wheels to go.

Steer the bike slowly.

And so the bike:

Feels more unstable and twitchy, with the front end sluggish and the rear too light.

Goes to places we don't want to.

Uses too much lean angle.

The first thing you need to do in the wet is relax. The front of the bike will track the road better if you don't have rigid 'broomstick' arms!

The second thing is to apply the throttle as soon as possible to make the bike more balanced, with roughly 40 per cent of the weight on the front and the rest on the rear.

The third thing is to look where there *is* grip, not to the places where there isn't – because you do go where you look.

## QUICK-TURNING IN THE WET

One of the benefits of being able to turn a bike quickly is that you can use less lean angle over more of the corner for a given speed. Therefore we all need to be able to quick-turn, especially in the wet when we want as much traction as possible. The more upright the bike, the better the grip in wet conditions. Wet-weather tyres have an extraordinary level of grip, so much so that you can still get your knee down in the rain. However, to keep lean angles sensible in the wet, some riders use a special wet-weather knee slider that's double the height of a normal one, thus ensuring that the bike doesn't lean over quite so far.

So, to make the bike turn more quickly in wet conditions we need to push the handlebar a little more quickly but not push it as quickly as we would in the dry. How far we push the bar dictates how far the bike will lean. How quickly or slowly we push the bar dictates how much lean we need to use for a corner. The slower the push, the slower the bike leans, the further we travel, the greater the lean angle – we have to lean over more to try and get the bike on line as it runs wide.

In the dry we can be really aggressive with how quickly we turn the bike. In the wet more finesse is required. It's harder to turn a bike quickly to 10 degrees of lean angle that it is to slap the thing on to your knee with 50 degrees of lean angle!

Valentino Rossi in full rain gear and looking comfortable. But talking of looking, he's the only MotoGP rider who'll wear a dark visor in all but the worst of wet conditions. And even then, as can be seen here, a tinted visor is used instead of a clear or even coloured (usually orange) rain visor.

Loris Capirossi chooses not to wear any waterproofs and is quite willing to get wet rather than have to put up with restrictive, additional clothing. This might be OK on a reasonably warm day, but in the cold the chill factor can be an issue. Despite the amount of standing water, he still has enough lean angle for his knee slider to be slicing through the water, such are the abilities of a wet-weather tyre.

A fear associated with quick turns is that you'll lose all front-end traction. It's not how quickly you turn a bike but how far you lean it that reduces the traction. As this is a wet-weather situation, we definitely don't want to be carrying lots of lean angle, so in theory the job should be easier!

## STEAMING VISORS

When the weather takes a turn for the worse and you ride in the rain, it seems that your visor steams up more readily. However, what's really happening is that you're holding your breath for longer because you're more tense on the bike when traction is reduced on wet tarmac.

The twist to this is that the tighter you hold the handlebars, the more likely you are to get into trouble – and then you'll be more likely to have difficulty seeing through a steamed-up visor because you've been holding your breath.

The visor problem results from holding your breath too long through a corner and then exhaling suddenly as you reach the end of the turn. The fogging is condensation caused by your warm breath meeting the cold surface of the visor. If you were to be more relaxed through the corner, you'd breathe more normally and the visor would remain clear. Once you can see where you're going, you'll feel more comfortable and therefore find it easier to relax.

**Dani Pedrosa with a high-tech Arai helmet designed to keep the visor clear in the rain. As well as having a tear-off visor to get rid of the muck and grime a wet race throws up, he has a mouth and nose guard to keep his warm breath away from the cold surface of the visor. Notice that the top of the visor also has a thin rubber strip to stop water running down the inside.**

**Sete Gibernau's clear upper rain suit wasn't enough to save him in this incident. The rain suit only covers the upper part of his body, suggesting that he finds the lowers too restrictive and doesn't mind getting wet feet and cold thighs. The upper part is clear so that the sponsors are still visible.**

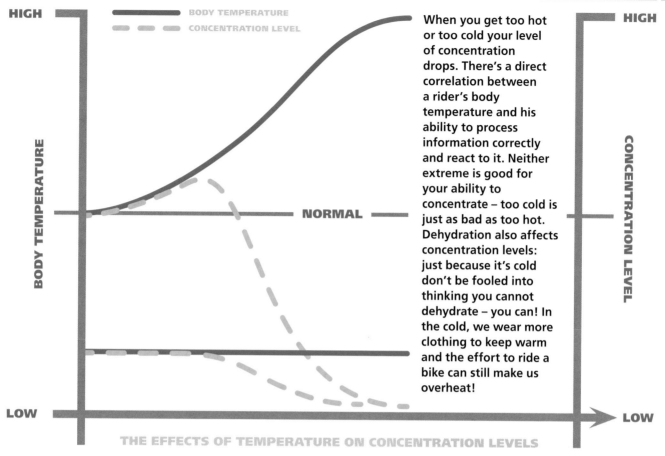

HIGH

BODY TEMPERATURE

CONCENTRATION LEVEL

BODY TEMPERATURE

NORMAL

CONCENTRATION LEVEL

HIGH

LOW

LOW

THE EFFECTS OF TEMPERATURE ON CONCENTRATION LEVELS

When you get too hot or too cold your level of concentration drops. There's a direct correlation between a rider's body temperature and his ability to process information correctly and react to it. Neither extreme is good for your ability to concentrate – too cold is just as bad as too hot. Dehydration also affects concentration levels: just because it's cold don't be fooled into thinking you cannot dehydrate – you can! In the cold, we wear more clothing to keep warm and the effort to ride a bike can still make us overheat!

## TEMPERATURE

It's not just the rain that can cause problems. The heat and the cold can take their toll too. Over the course of a season MotoGP racers have to face the extreme heat of the Losail circuit in Qatar, the cold wind at Phillip Island in Australia, the humidity of the air at Sepang in Malaysia, and the dampness often experienced at Donington Park in the UK. They need to be able to deal with extremes of climate.

The temperature of the desert in Qatar can get extremely high. In 2005 it reached 48 degrees on the track surface, but the riders still had to get around the circuit as fast as possible. Even in a temperate climate, riding a bike is hard work as you use a great deal of energy and the heat build-up in your leathers can be considerable. This is why professional riders wear leathers with perforations and stretch panels that allow some airflow around their bodies to help stay cool.

In the heat of the desert, riders must ensure that they not only keep their water levels high but also get a lot of salt and potassium, two minerals that help the body to absorb water. Without them water simply passes straight through the body – you could drink eight litres of water and actually absorb only a fraction of it. Bananas and ready-salted crisps provide the salt

Riding a MotoGP bike in hot weather is hard work as ruddy-faced James Ellison illustrates. This isn't a sign that he's unfit in any way – it's just that some of the countries visited by the MotoGP circus have high heat and humidity that can sap the energy of the fittest riders in the paddock.

and potassium just as well as any water additives you can buy. Watch for signs of dehydration: a headache is the first, and loss of concentration goes hand in hand with this.

Some MotoGP riders now have a Camelbak-type arrangement that sits in the hump on the back of the leathers. This small bladder allows the rider to drink while he's out on the track.

"I drink a shit load of water, man," says Colin Edwards. "I'm not one to take supplements and vitamins and all that crap. As long as I'm hydrated then I'm good. I just drink lots of water."

In the humidity of Malaysia the dehydration problem is just the same, but even the perforations in a rider's leathers do little to help. One of the biggest problems is perspiration, as beads of sweat can run down the forehead and into the eyes. In the past many riders used to put a sanitary towel on the inside of the helmet to absorb sweat, but nowadays helmet manufacturers have more sophisticated variations on the theme. Venting in the shell of the lid also helps to provide airflow over the rider's head as a further aid to keeping cool.

In Australia the sea winds blowing across Phillip Island make the place feel cold, even when the sun's out. Because the sponsors naturally want their logos fully visible, the riders cannot do as we would and simply put a jacket over the top of their leathers. To help keep the cold out and the heat in, it's possible to obtain leathers that are unperforated but this isn't always an option on a race weekend. Other choices to keep warm are to wear a thin windproof bib or to put on another layer underneath the leathers. The ideal is an inner suit that's thin enough to fit underneath without making tight spots around the joints. This could restrict blood flow and cause distraction, or, worse still, make the hands, arms, feet or legs numb.

In the wet the need to keep the rider warm is just as important as keeping him dry. In the past a lightweight oversuit used to do the job, but this kind of garment is loose-fitting and flaps around too much in the wind. The material also allows the rider to slip around on the seat and makes it harder for him to lock into the fuel tank under braking and cornering.

In recent years, however, we've seen the arrival of clear outer suits that fit closely to the leathers. Made from a Latex-type material, this kind of suit closely hugs the rider, keeping him both warm and dry. The stretchy nature of the suit also allows the rider to move around freely. Some outer suits even have holes in the knees for the sliders to fit through so that a rider can

**1** Perforated leathers help to keep a flow of air through most of the rider's body. This works well in Europe but can be too much in the heat of Qatar!

**2** The inner suit material can be made to help absorb sweat – a good idea as no rider wants to develop sweat and heat sores over a race weekend.

**3** The liner seen here is of the CoolMax type, again designed to mop up sweat. Most riders now have a separate inner suit made of the same material. This allows the rider to slide his leathers off at the end of a ride rather than having them stick to his sweaty body.

**4** The ventilation even extends down the legs, the back of the thighs and the calf muscles. The stretch panels also allow airflow around the rider's body.

"I DRINK A SHIT LOAD OF WATER, MAN. I'M NOT ONE TO TAKE SUPPLEMENTS AND VITAMINS AND ALL THAT CRAP. AS LONG AS I'M HYDRATED THEN I'M GOOD. I JUST DRINK LOTS OF WATER."
**COLIN EDWARDS**

In the desert or in the rain, keeping your fluid levels high is important as this helps to maintain concentration. Drink as much as possible, as you'll lose a lot of fluid during a race or track day. Eating pasta and bananas also helps keep energy levels high towards the end of a race or track day.

still guage his lean angle without destroying a set of waterproofs.

You can be the best wet-weather rider in the world, but if you get too cold out there on the bike you'll find it difficult to use the controls. You'll also find it difficult to maintain a high level of concentration, and that in turn will make it difficult to stay on the bike. The same applies if you get too hot: you can again lose concentration and this can lead to a mistake, so regulate your temperature and keep hydrated.

# CONSERVING

Don't overstress the machine, tyres or yourself – ride only fast enough to win

When your tyre looks like this, you know you've been pushing hard – very hard. The rider who used this tyre would have been suffering quite badly from a lack of traction towards the end of his race. If it were a qualifying tyre, the chances are the rider would have set a circuit record!

Spinning the rear tyre looks cool and is good fun – and it's a valid racing technique. When you first start to push this hard, it'll take a lot of your attention, mental as well as physical. It'll take a while before you can do it comfortably and at will. When you reach this stage, though, you'll be able to do it all day long. Your lap times wouldn't be much good – but what fun!

Shinya Nakano getting ready to ride. Riders don't have a chair in the garage just because they're lazy – they relax to conserve energy before another session on the bike. If you've done ten laps at 100 per cent in practice or qualifying and there's still 15 minutes to go, you need to conserve your energy the better. If you don't have a chair when you go racing or to a track day – get one!

The higher you rise through the tree of racing, the longer the races tend to become. At club level you'll be faced with 10 minutes of practice followed by two or three races of about six laps. The next stage is to move up to national level: although there'll be variations from country to country, in general you'll have more time to practise and the races will get longer. And if you were to make it into MotoGP, you'd have three hours of practice time, one hour of qualifying time, half an hour of free practice on race day, and then the race itself – all spread over three days. Or you could go down the endurance route, where you might be riding for an hour or more at a time at nearly full pace, for a day.

It's a good idea, therefore, to learn how to keep getting the best from your machine, including the suspension and tyres – and not burning up or burning out any components. As a general rule if one part fails, then the whole bike will fail too.

Valentino Rossi likes to keep things to a minimum: "Riding is very much about all your movement on the motorcycle. The bike feels every move you make – the braking, the throttle and your movement to steer the bike. To have everything under control is better to ride smooth. Maybe with little bikes, like 125s, it's possible to be more aggressive. But on more heavy bikes – like a MotoGP bike or 1000cc street bike, you need to

ride smooth by making all your movements very smooth. If you ride too aggressive you will lose stability."

In a race, even in a short, sharp club race, there's going to be a need to conserve yourself, your bike and your tyres. The longer the race, the easier it becomes to manage these elements, but even in a short eight-lapper you'll need to keep a watchful eye on yourself and your bike.

Whether you win a race by 10 seconds or one tenth of a second, a win is still a win. This is a good thing to keep remembering while you're in the heat of competition.

You'll also need to take this into account on a track day. OK, speeds at a track day will very likely be slower, but you'll still have a lot of riding to do throughout the day – and conserving your energy and concentration is just as important.

When you're getting ready on race day morning, you'll undoubtedly have the odd jolt of adrenaline, or even a constant stream of it. This sets the heart racing and marks the beginning of a long day that'll definitely be tiring, although you may not realise it until the end of the day when the rush of adrenaline has gone – and you collapse in a heap in the van on the way home.

Endurance, stamina, call it what you will, is going to help – which is why gym training is good for you (see the *Preparation* chapter).

"IN THE RACE YOU RIDE
AT 95 PER CENT. IT IS
NOT POSSIBLE TO RIDE
AT 100 PER CENT FOR
ALL OF THE RACE."
LORIS CAPIROSSI

Dani Pedrosa and Nicky Hayden riding to their limits as well as those of their bikes and tyres. The rider who can conserve his tyres until the last part of the race will have more options open to him than the man who burns them up in the first few laps. Taking care of your grip levels while still riding fast is an art all of its own.

Always bear in mind what's ahead of you through the day. Although you'll be concentrating race by race or session by session, you'll also need to look at the bigger picture. I know of one track day addict who never goes out in the final session because he's afraid of making a mistake while trying too hard in 'the last one of the day.' It's a somewhat flawed plan, though, as *your* final session of the day will always be just that, even if it's not everyone else's! During a race meeting, of course, this isn't a luxury available to you...

Make sure you rest as much as possible between races or track sessions. Having a chair for chilling out is an excellent idea and a vital item for your packing list, along with tools, water and copious amounts of chocolate for that carb and sugar 'hit' throughout the day.

Don't eat too much in one go. It's better to be a 'grazer' and nibble lots of little things through the day. It's a sad but true fact that most crashes

Race engines are highly tuned and highly stressed, and if you give them too much abuse they'll let you know by letting go. Here Carlos Checa has done just that and the engine on his Yamaha has finally let him know in a big cloud of smoke. Engine conservation is aided by having it rebuilt on a regular basis.

at track days occur during the first session after lunch or the last session of the day. The former is due to reduced concentration after a meal, the latter due to fatigue after a hard day.

When on track there are several elements that you need to conserve. Tyres are the first, either because you want to get more race meetings or track days out of them to keep your budget under control, or – at a higher level – because you need a soft tyre to last through a whole race. Either way, if you go flat-stick from the off and right through the race, you'll find grip a problem sooner or later.

As Loris Capirossi says: "In the race you ride at 95 per cent. It is not possible to ride at 100 per cent for all of the race."

Be relaxed. Conserving mental and physical energy will be down to how relaxed you can be on the bike. The more relaxed you feel and the more relaxed you are, the longer you'll last and the higher your concentration level will be towards the end of the day.

If you hang on to your bike's handlebars with a death grip in the first session of the day, with gritted teeth and holding your breath in each corner, and you'll be exhausted in next to no time. Forearm pump will prevail (see the *Braking* chapter), as will upper body aches and pains.

"With these bikes," states Nicky Hayden, "the

**As well as conserving our energy, we also need to conserve our tyres so that they last the race. This will involve choosing the right compound of tyre to last the distance.**

**Basically there are three compounds, although the issue can be further complicated by using different compounds front and rear, and different profiles, wheel sizes, tyre and rim widths – as well as the condition of the track surface.**

**A hard compound won't provide as much grip initially but will offer more consistent grip over a race distance.**

**A soft compound will have much more grip at the beginning of a race but will fade off quickly as the race progresses and might not even go the whole distance.**

**A medium compound, therefore, gives you a compromise position somewhere in between.**

HIGH

GRIP LEVEL

LOW

—————— HARD-COMPOUND TYRE

– – – – MEDIUM-COMPOUND TYRE

– – – – SOFT-COMPOUND TYRE

START OF RACE

END OF RACE

front wheel is in the air most of the time so you can't really pull on the bars. So you actually grip the tank and pull and push your body with your legs."

Ironically, if you're more relaxed you'll also give the bike, the engine and the tyres an easier time. Operating the bike's controls – throttle, brakes, gears, steering – with less aggression and more smoothness will put less wear and tear on all the component parts of the bike. Engine, tyres, brake pads, suspension components, chain – everything will last longer.

Of all those parts, the tyres are going to be the most important in a racing situation. You'll want to run the softest combination possible to give you that outright grip, but at the same time you'll need a compound that'll last the race. It's no good fitting a qualifier and getting off to a flying start for the first few laps if you're just going to get reeled in and then overtaken by your rivals when your super-sticky tyres go off, leaving you sliding while the others are driving.

Mind you, if you could establish a sufficiently big advantage in

those first few laps, it might be another story. Wayne Rainey used this strategy on more than one occasion, but it requires extremely good management of your sliding once the tyre has gone off.

Even if you have the best set of brakes that the rules allow, you can still be too hard on them – unless you have carbon brakes. You can start to lose braking power during the course of a race or even overheat them on some tracks. When the brakes do fade, you'll find that the brake lever comes back to the handlebar and your ability to slow down becomes less and less effective. Braking a little earlier and less hard will help to make sure the brakes last the whole race. It's that 95 per cent thing all over again...

Racing is a study in conservation. How many times have you seen a rider come on strong at the end of a race and gain several positions because he cleverly paced himself, his bike and his tyres right from the very start?

When I was competing, I recall one race at Mallory Park where I made an absolute blinder of a start and had nearly half the track as a lead by the end of the first lap. But I'd burned the tyre within two laps, and slowly I lost places as I struggled for grip...

Get the idea?

Can you apply the **'I'M SAFE'** rule as used by private light aircraft pilots?

I     **INFECTION**
M    **MEDICATION**
S     **SLEEP**
A     **ALCOHOL**
F     **FOOD**
E     **EMOTION**

Tackling these points one by one...

Do you have an **INFECTION** that will reduce your ability to process information when riding quickly? A heavy cold, flu, a stomach upset – you name it. Any infection will impinge on your riding. This applies to the best of them and will seriously hinder your abilities.

**MEDICATION** Are you taking drugs? Will they make you drowsy and slow down your reaction times? Will they mask a problem that should really be dealt with in another manner?

Have you had enough **SLEEP**? As the road signs say, 'Tiredness can kill'. If you're tired, you won't be operating at 100 per cent. Adrenaline can only overcome so many shortcomings and ultimately it can be rendered ineffective.

**ALCOHOL** After drinking, you might ride faster because you're less aware of what's going on around you. You could also hurt someone. And hurt yourself. Don't do it.

**FOOD** When you eat a heavy or large meal, you lose concentration and can feel sleepy. Just think of Grandad at Christmas in front of the telly, jaw wide open, snoring and dribbling through the Queen's Speech!

A lot of accidents occur on track days just after lunch. When you eat, your body needs to digest the food you've just forced into your stomach and to complete this action it needs blood. The biggest hog of blood on a track day is your brain because you've been using it all morning and now your tummy's going to nick a lot of it in order to get rid of the heavy track burger you've just eaten. This means your concentration will definitely have dropped from its level in the morning. Not surprising to learn, then, that riders forget they haven't been on track for over an hour during the lunch break and their tyres have cooled down...

Have something light to eat and take an extra lap or two to warm up your tyres.

And **EMOTION** It's not a good idea to go for a fast ride when you've just had a massive row with the bank manager, wife, girlfriend or parents. Or if you have something weighing on your mind, a distraction of some description, whatever the cause.

Do you have enough concentration left to be able to read your pit board as you pass it at over 100mph? If you cannot see your pit board, you're starting to run into a problem and should probably call it a day.

# WINNING

How to stay on top
of the rostrum

It's all about getting over the line first. But even if you don't win, beating another rider after a race-long battle is still a very good feeling. Racers are a competitive bunch with huge egos – this is part of the attitude needed to race. And even if you don't win, a good position in the points can be just as vital to winning a championship.

Staying on top is probably harder than the first time you win, either in a race or a championship. This was never truer to me than when my wife won the Eskrima stick-fighting world championship in LA in 1996. She'd won the British title twice, the European title twice and then the single- and double-stick World titles. When I asked her if she was going to defend her title the following year she replied: "No. I've reached the top and the only way now is down. I want to finish at the top of the game."

So when someone like Valentino Rossi, Mick Doohan or Wayne Rainey clocks up yet another championship title with little threat from the opposition, where does that motivation come from? To do it time and time again? It could be understood if there was a strong challenge every year, year after year, but in 500cc and in MotoGP it hasn't really been the case for these riders. So what's the key?

Loris Capirossi has been in the GP paddock since he was 17 and he agrees that the single biggest thing a rider has to deal with is the pressure. He believes that young riders of 14 and 15 need to be helped to deal with the pressure.

After Thomas Lüthi won the 125cc World Championship in 2005, the pressure of defending his title in 2006 had a huge effect not only on him but also the team around him. When you're successful in racing, the pressure to continue to do well is huge, but luckily not insurmountable.

Once a rider gets back to winning ways after a lean spell, the whole team can rejoice and revel in the moment. But whether it's a single race win, your first championship points, your first finish or just crossing the line, the satisfaction will be short-lived. The next race will bring a new set of challenges to overcome.

Thomas Lüthi won the 125cc World Championship in 2005, and his experience shows that the pressure of being a champion really doesn't become apparent until the time comes to defend the title the following year. The pressure a rider has to cope with as a reigning champion is particularly high.

The pressure on his shoulders to repeat the same form the following season was huge. Some of the pressure came from himself, some from the media and some from the perceived expectations of his fans. He was the 125cc World Champion in 2005 and he was racing in the same class for 2006 – so it seemed that he should be winning everything.

As his riding coach, I believe that this pressure led to him making a few mistakes in the IRTA tests in 2006, with the result that he crashed and broke his collarbone – his first serious injury for over a year. This took time to heal, and the pressure continued during that period. It was really only after he won the French GP at Le Mans (for the second successive year) that he felt the pressure ease off. Back to winning ways – and the whole mood of the team, the media and the fans lifted.

At the time of writing, just after that GP, everyone involved with him was looking forward to the next race at Mugello in Italy just two weeks later – and hoping the result was a good one!

## AND JUST ONE THING I WOULD LIKE TO IMPROVE...

■ "There is not one thing I can say I want to do better – not braking, nothing, because I think I'm the best anyway at everything. You have to think that way to be a racer in the first place. You are always trying to improve everything." *Colin Edwards*

■ "It would be to become a bit braver on the brakes. I never have been a great late-braker." *James Ellison*

■ "To be more efficient on the bike so I don't make so many movements to make the bike work." *Chris Vermeulen*

■ "Being more focused on exiting properly and faster." *Chaz Davies*

■ "More consistent throughout the entire race, to cut back on the little mistakes and slow it down a little bit by the apex of the corner and get better drive out." *John Hopkins*

■ "Braking, erm, braking, yes, braking." *Shinya Nakano*

■ "That in every race my bike is good enough to win the race." *Thomas Lüthi*

The most successful racer of all time? Valentino Rossi continues to retain the motivation to keep winning because there are always new challenges for him to face. At the time of writing he has young newcomers like Casey Stoner and Dani Pedrosa presenting the new challenge.

## THE MotoGP POINTS SYSTEM

Points are awarded from first to 15th place inclusive, and a running total is kept until after the last race of the season. The rider with the most points after the last race wins the championship.

|  |  |
|---|---|
| 1st | **25 points** |
| 2nd | **20 points** |
| 3rd | **16 points** |
| 4th | **13 points** |
| 5th | **11 points** |
| 6th | **10 points** |
| 7th | **9 points** |
| 8th | **8 points** |
| 9th | **7 points** |
| 10th | **6 points** |
| 11th | **5 points** |
| 12th | **4 points** |
| 13th | **3 points** |
| 14th | **2 points** |
| 15th | **1 point** |

# SUSPENSION EDUCATION PROGRAM

This suspension discovery checklist was developed by Keith Code for California Superbike School students

The rear spring of a bike (or any vehicle for that matter) is designed to keep the rear wheel in contact with the ground as much as possible. The spring is preloaded so that it will drop the wheel into any holes or dips. However, too much and the spring will require greater and greater forces to get it to move. Setting your spring sag has a huge effect on the bike's stability.

Suspension: it's full of loopholes, contradictions and pub experts. And if there's one thing that will help you to the top of the tree then it's an understanding of what it can and can't do, and it's how you read it that makes the difference. There's more misinformation about what this bike needs or how that bike should be set up than about any other part of motorcycle racing.

There's no ideal setting for any given machine. Every bike to come out of Japan, Italy or any other country in the world has a setting or set-up that's a compromise. When a bike rolls off the production line, it has to be able to cope with riders who are tall, riders who are short, those who hang off and those who don't, those who square corners off and those who use a classic line, riders who are big-boned and those who weigh less than a wet sparrow. And the bike must handle reasonably well with all these riders and combination of styles, and this is even before we go down the road of poor throttle control and excessive or inappropriate rider input.

Just for the record, most handling problems come from you, and so, before you even think about getting the spanners out, you should make sure you're relaxed on the bike in the turn, not giving unwanted handlebar input, and you have good throttle control because the throttle can cause, and also cure, all sorts of problems. Roll on and off in a corner and you will know exactly what we mean, and we know you've done that more than once in your riding career!

The real key to suspension set-up is in tailoring the bike to you and your riding style and abilities. What works for one racer won't work for you.

You need to educate yourself so that you can make an informed and accurate decision on exactly what the bike needs to make it suit your style.

The 'Suspension Education Program' was designed by coaching guru Keith Code of California Superbike School fame to help you learn what too much rebound will feel like, what too little sag does for the bike and how to unlock the key to handling nirvana.

Like all good training programs, you do one little thing at a time until you have felt what each drill does to your bike. With this information you will then be able to adjust your own suspension to suit and know if and when you need a re-valve, new shock, springs or just a tad more front compression damping.

We are assuming here that you have good tyres, suspension that actually works (has damping), good headstock bearings, the chain correctly tensioned and swing arm bearings greased and working. If not then stop wasting your time and get them fixed.

## SAG

This is the most important part of correct suspension set-up and it comes in two parts. Most of you will know that setting the static sag is vital, but few riders realise that this is only half of the drill. You need to set both the static *and* rider sag to see if you have the right strength springs fitted to the front and rear of your bike. The correct spring means that, in most cases, the middle third of the travel will be used. This is the most efficient range of the shock since it leaves enough travel at both the top and bottom of the stroke to deal with all that the track or rider can throw at it.

Remember that it's the spring that does all the work; the shock is just there to control the spring.

## SETTING STATIC SAG

To make sure that the springs, both front and rear, are able to work in this middle third we need to see how much the bike settles under its own weight. This is the basic static sag.

To get a true reading, we first need to set all the damping settings to minimum, so that the spring can fully extend without the damping holding it back. With a screwdriver, or using the knobs on the shock, count how many clicks or turns it takes to wind the damping fully in. This gives you your original settings should it all go wrong and you want to go back to how it felt before. You wind the damping adjusters in because we should always count from fully in to fully out and not the other way round. This is because there is always some slack when the damping is wound all the way out, making a correct count of turns or clicks near impossible.

Write these settings down on a sheet of paper and then wind all the damping off, compression and rebound, both front and rear.

Now, with the aid of a friend, pull the bike over on its side stand (Ducati owners would be better with two friends lifting the front of the bike with the handlebars as the stand is weak) and measure the amount they have extended. This is easy on upside-downers as you just measure the exposed chrome or titanium nitrate. On 'normal' forks measure from the bottom of the lower yoke to the top of the fork leg. Write this measurement down. It will always remain the same and it's your base measurement.

Now let the bike back down, bounce the front end a couple of times to let it settle and then measure again. The difference between the two figures is your front static sag.

For a road bike you should look for 30 to 40mm. For a race bike you should look for 15 to 25mm.

Now you need to do the rear. Again, lift the rear of the bike off the ground and measure from the middle of the rear wheel spindle to a place directly above it. You may need to make a mark on the under tray to measure from. If you have a hollow wheel spindle then it's better to measure from the top of the hole. Write this figure down as this will be your rear base measurement. Now let the bike back down, bounce the rear a couple of times to let it settle and then measure again. The difference between the two figures is your rear static sag.

For a road bike you should look for 15 to 25mm. For a race bike you should look for 0 to 10mm.

Before you get your tools out, get your lid and go and ride a few laps to gauge how the bike feels with no damping and the springs set as they are now. When you get back write down how it felt. Words like 'awful', 'frightening' and 'pogo' are acceptable. This is your own base setting or, to be more accurate, feeling.

Now we are going to check the rider sag. You will need someone to steady the bike and someone to take the measurements while you get on board. Bounce on the foot pegs a few times and allow the bike to settle with you adopting your normal riding position. Don't hold

the front brake on while doing this as it will stop the bike from settling fully.

Now repeat the measurements for the front and rear, taking the figure away from the base measurement. You will be looking for the following measurements:

■ **FRONT**
For a road bike: 35 to 50mm
For a race bike: 25 to 35mm
■ **REAR**
For a road bike: 30 to 45mm
For a race bike: 20 to 25mm

If you can get in the static range but outside the rider range (over 35mm race front) then the spring is too soft.

If you can get in the static range but inside the rider range (under 25mm race front) then the spring is too hard.

If you can't get in the rider range then the spring needs changing.

Once you have got into these ranges, or as near as possible, it's time to put your lid on again and go and ride a few more laps. You will be amazed at the difference just this small part of the program makes. Come back and write down what you felt.

Sag is the amount the spring will travel under the weight of the bike and with the weight of the bike and rider combined. Static sag refers to the amount the springs, front and rear, will compress under the weight of the bike. Rider sag is the amount the springs will compress with a rider on board the bike. The difference between these two figures will tell you if you have the right strength of spring fitted.

REAR SAG

FRONT SAG

# DAMPING

### ■ STAGE ONE

Now we need a screwdriver. Adjust your front compression damping to full, all the way in. The compression is the bottom screw near the front wheel spindle.

Go and ride. When you get back, write down how it felt. This will give you a record to refer to when you want to fine-tune your settings.

### ■ STAGE TWO

Set the compression back to zero and dial the front rebound to the maximum. Go and ride and once more write down what you felt.

### ■ STAGE THREE

Set the rebound back to zero and dial the rear compression to its maximum. It's the knob or screw on the remote reservoir. Go and ride and once more write down what you felt.

### ■ STAGE FOUR

Set the compression back to zero and dial the rear rebound to the maximum. It's the knob or screw on the bottom of the shock and can be difficult to get to on some bikes. Go and ride and once more write down what you felt.

These things that you feel are going to tell you what you need to adjust if you get a problem with the handling of your bike. You may well be surprised to find that the rear setting creates a feeling at the front of the bike and vice versa.

Now it's time to refine your new-found knowledge and see if you can still pick the feelings out when there are other damping forces in place.

Put all the damping settings to the halfway.

### ■ STAGE FIVE

Adjust your front compression damping to full, all the way in. Leave the others at halfway.

Get out there and ride. Come back and write it down again. The same feeling will be there but more subtle, a little harder to nail down.

### ■ STAGE SIX

Set the compression back to half way and dial the front rebound to the max. Go and ride and once more write down what you felt.

### ■ STAGE SEVEN

Set the rebound back to halfway and dial the rear compression to the max. Ride. How did it feel?

### ■ STAGE EIGHT

Set the compression back to halfway and dial the rear rebound to the max. We're nearly there. How did it feel?

By now you should have a good idea of what too much or too little of any of the settings feels like. You should know which feeling created at the front actually comes from the rear and so on. There is no right or wrong answer to what you have felt. What's important is that you have felt a difference in all the settings, so now you can make educated adjustments to get the bike to handle as you want it to.

### ■ Final test

Set all the damping to halfway. Go and ride. Is it what you want or can you now make the small and correct adjustments to suit? You should be able to because you have been educated in the feelings. It's no longer a mystery or black art. You can now do what the good MotoGP racers do and come back to the pits and get your mechanics to make good adjustments. Just remember that you must have good throttle control and a loose upper body so the bike can work properly through any given corner.

## A NOTE ON RIDE HEIGHT

The main reason to change a bike's ride height is to alter the steering geometry of the bike to either help it to turn more quickly or become more stable. More ride height quickens the steering, but makes the bike less stable and reduces rear grip under power. Less ride height slows the steering, but makes the bike more stable and increases rear grip under power.

Here are a few symptoms of changing your ride height:

**Too much ride height will give you:**
High-speed instability
Poor rear grip
Instability under heavy braking

**Too little ride height will give you:**
Understeer on corner exit
Difficulty in changing direction
Poor front-end grip on exit

The front fork springs sit inside the fork tubes. The adjuster on the top adds more or less preload and inside this adjuster is another one for setting the rebound damping. A good front stand that sits under the bottom yoke will be needed to replace the springs if required.

# AUTHOR ACKNOWLEDGEMENTS

First and foremost to Keith Code, riding guru to more World Champions than anyone else in the world and founder of the California Superbike School – a place where more champions have been, heard about, talked about and read about than any other. Without his training, insight and support, it wouldn't have been possible for me to write this book, nor would I have been able to coach Thomas Lüthi to his 125cc World Championship title in 2005.

To Julian Ryder and Haynes Publishing for the opportunity to write this book and to get to talk to all of the best riders on this fair planet.

To all the racers who were willing to talk to me honestly and openly about their riding, to agree, contradict, enlighten and amaze me. Make no mistake: these racers enjoy going fast, enjoy competing, and enjoy the best bikes ever built. So, in alphabetical order: Leon Camier, Loris Capirossi, Chaz Davies, Colin Edwards, James Ellison, Nicky Hayden, John Hopkins, Thomas Lüthi, Shinya Nakano and Chris Vermeulen. Valentino Rossi's views were supplied by Mat Oxley.

To the crew at the California Superbike School in the UK: Johnny, Donna, Lynn, Paul, Glenn, Steve and all our Riding Coaches here and abroad for their support, directly, indirectly, sometimes blunt, always honest and for the endless banter, may it never stop.

To Colin Schiller, who gave me the chance to enter the world of bike journalism and test riding when no-one else would even open the door and give a video store manager the chance to prove what he could do.

My Mum and Dad for being proud of their son and to my sisters who never know where I'm going to be next and for putting up with me missing their birthdays.

Finally, to my lovely wife Donna and my beautiful two sons Kit and Alfie who tolerate Daddy spending a lot of time away from home, in his office writing, sometimes cursing, always grumpy but never kicking the cats.

"THERE ARE ONLY THREE SPORTS: BULLFIGHTING, MOTOR RACING & MOUNTAINEERING. ALL THE REST ARE MERELY GAMES."

**ATTRIBUTED TO ERNEST HEMINGWAY**